Eric David Dawson CEO and co-founder of 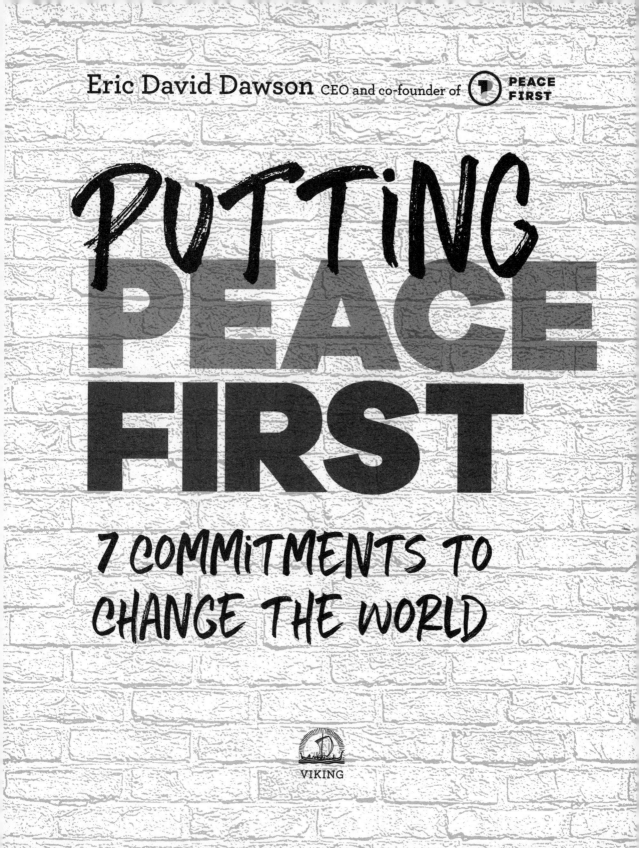 PEACE FIRST

PUTTING PEACE FIRST

7 COMMITMENTS TO CHANGE THE WORLD

VIKING

VIKING
An imprint of Penguin Random House LLC
375 Hudson Street
New York, New York 10014

First published in the United States of America by Viking,
an imprint of Penguin Random House LLC, 2018

All quotations are from interviews conducted by the author either in person, via telephone, or by email between April 21, 2014, and September 8, 2016.

LIBRARY OF CONGRESS CATALOGING-IN-PUBLICATION DATA IS AVAILABLE
ISBN 9781101997338

Printed in U.S.A.   Set in Archer   Book design by Kate Renner

10 9 8 7 6 5 4 3 2 1

Photo credits:
Contents page: Photo by Marcus Williams. Used with permission from Peace First; 3: © Peace First; 6: Photo by Claire Lawlor. Used with permission from Peace First; 13: Photo courtesy Alaa Aissi, Associated Students of University of California; 16: Photo courtesy Life Academy Team. Used with permission from Peace First; 23 and 26: Photos courtesy The BE ONE Project. Used with permission from Peace First; 27, 49, 66, and 87: Photos by Dalton Bentley. © Peace First; 35: Photo provided by Mike Ekern/University of St. Thomas School of Law; 39: Photo by Nancy Schwindel. Used with permission from Peace First; 40: Photo by Paul Middlestaedt, courtesy College of St. Benedict; 47: Photo courtesy Wei Chen. Used with permission from Peace First; 52: Photo by Harvey Finkle. Used with permission from Peace First; 61: Photo by Rich Schmitt Photography. © Peace First; 65: Photo courtesy Jeremiah Anthony. © Peace First; 73: Photo by Zoë Gewanter-Reznick. Used with permission from Peace First; 77: Photo by Rebecca Yenawine. Used with permission from Peace First; 85: Photo by Julian Baptiste du Buclet. © Peace First; 89: Photo courtesy Think Twice Campaign. Used with permission from Peace First; 90: Photo by Sarah Cofrin. © Peace First.

To Mom, Dad, and Tammy for giving me roots

To Francelia, Steven, and Anne for giving me wings

To Xochitl, Jivan, and Veronica for giving me hope

Peacemaker Marcus Williams reading his book, The Stop Bullying Club, *to a group of young students.*

CONTENTS

Prologue: *Confessions of an Angry Kid* 1

Introduction: *You've Been Lied To* 4

Peacemaker Manifesto 8

Commitment 1: *Put Peace First, Every Day* 12

Commitment 2: *Raise My Hand* 22

Commitment 3: *Open My Heart* 34

Commitment 4: *Take a Stand* 46

Commitment 5: *Bring Others Along* 60

Commitment 6: *Work with My Enemies* 72

Commitment 7: *Keep Trying* 84

Putting It Together 99

Epilogue: *Pending Disasters* 137

Acknowledgments 141

Index 144

CONFESSIONS OF AN ANGRY KID

I WAS A pretty angry kid. Not a get-in-a-lot-of-fights kind of angry, but angry nonetheless. The world felt unfair to me. Adults often let me down or dismissed my ideas. I attended high school at a time when students with disabilities were no longer being kept in separate classrooms but joining the rest of the school for most of the day—gym, lunch, health class. Often, because they were different, these students were tormented, made fun of, and bullied. This made me even angrier.

I wasn't alone in my anger. There were other students who shared my concern and we began organizing to change this. We started with a few workshops and trainings for our fellow students. We brought in speakers and held fundraisers. Most importantly, we made a commitment to intervene whenever we saw bad things happening in the cafeteria or hallway, to stand up for other people. We made it clear to our peers that certain behaviors were not OK. It made a difference. The bullying stopped. Not because the principal or teachers made a new rule but because we changed the culture of our school, student to student. I felt powerful, like I could make good things happen, even though I was young.

When I started college, I wanted other young people to believe they could make a difference too. I found friends who felt the same way and we began volunteering in local elementary schools, teaching students how to create their own projects to make their schools or neighborhoods better. What started in a dorm room twenty-five years ago is now a global nonprofit called Peace First, which has supported hundreds of thousands of young people all over the globe, helping them to be brave and kind, and to launch their own projects to solve problems. This book is a collection of all I have learned about how young people can change the world for the better—not someday, but right now—through everyday choices and by working together to tackle larger injustices.

Think of this book as a how-to guide for making the world a better place based on seven key commitments for becoming a better person. Each commitment chapter shares the story of a real young person who has tackled a significant problem and made it better. Exercises at the end of each of these stories will deepen your thinking and help you plan out how to follow through on this commitment every day. After these commitment chapters comes a step-by-step guide for creating your own project. My hope is that this book will not only serve as an inspiration for what you can do, but that it will help you choose to do it every day.

Because it is our daily choices that ultimately matter. There is a parable that's often credited to the Cherokee people about a grandfather and his grandson. A child approaches his grandfather, who is visibly upset. "Grandfather," he asks, "what is wrong?" "My son," the grandfather replies, "I feel like I have these two wolves fighting inside of me. One wolf is vengeful, angry, and violent. The other wolf is loving, peaceful, and kind. They are at war inside my spirit." The grandson thinks about this for a moment, then, turning to his grandfather, he asks, "Which of these two wolves do you think will win?" To which the grandfather replies, "Whichever wolf I choose to feed."

I wrote this book for anyone who wants to feed the good in themselves and in the world.

I wrote this book for anyone who, like I did, is growing up angry. For whom the world feels particularly unfair, and who wants to channel their frustration into something good, something powerful.

I wrote this for anyone who sees what is broken in the world and has no idea where to start fixing it. Those who see the world not just as it is but how it could be, and want to act.

I wrote this book for the artists and creators who are ready to imagine new possibilities and want to use their talents to invite others along.

I wrote this book for those who are not always the first to raise their hand but have good ideas; for those whom people tend to overlook because they are not the loudest or the funniest or the fastest.

For all young people who want to to help, I wrote this book for you.

The author, at age 20, leading a peacemaker training.

YOU'VE BEEN LiED TO

YOU ARE THE FUTURE.

The scene could be from any assembly at any school anywhere in the world. An inspirational speaker, sweating in the bright lights of the auditorium, explaining how important you will be . . . someday. It seems from the moment you are born, adults are talking about your bright future. How with hard work, focus, and determination you will be a great writer, athlete, leader, teacher, artist—whatever—someday. How at some distant point in the future you will change the world.

This is a lie.

You are not the future. You are the present. You do not need to wait for some magical *someday* when all of a sudden you will have learned enough, read enough, become ready enough to make a difference. No. You can be great right now. And in many ways you are the best hope we have for fixing a world divided by fear, hatred, and violence.

Not someday. Right now.

But how?

There are tons of ways to make the world a better place. When we listen to a friend share about their hard day or take a moment to pick up a piece of trash in a park. When we walk for a cause and when we offer our seat to a stranger. We make a difference when we work to understand someone else's point of view and when we volunteer our time in shelters and food pantries. In fact, there are so many ways to make a difference that it can be overwhelming. Can it ever be enough? And where do you even start?

The best place to start is with yourself. Adults often ask young people, "*What* do you want to do when you grow up?" but rarely, "*Who* do you want to be?" And that is by far the more important question. Our beliefs, our values, those things we hold dear in our hearts determine how we act in the world. Who you are matters. And you will make a difference, not just by the things that you *do* but by *who* you are while you do them.

We tend to think changing the world is done by BIG IMPORTANT people at BIG IMPORTANT moments, when in fact the world is always changed by regular people deciding to be different. The civil rights movement wasn't just important speeches and a few key leaders. It was hundreds of thousands of people, often young people, deciding they were going to be different—kinder, braver, more inclusive—through small choices made each and every day. So if you want to change the world, the best place to start is with yourself and those commitments you make to help other people.

Joining our commitments with others is how we solve our world's biggest problems. If we are going to do anything worthwhile to create better and fairer communities—to end violence, protect our environment, improve our schools, ensure everyone has enough food to eat and a place to sleep—the single most powerful act we must do is commit each and every day to being audacious problem-solvers. **TO BEING PEACEMAKERS.**

Peace can be a difficult idea to wrap your hands around. It can seem passive—being weak and letting others take advantage of you. It can feel soft and fuzzy—sitting in a quiet meadow, holding hands and singing songs. It is often defined by what it is not—no conflicts and fewer weapons. And it can seem unattainable—needing to measure up to iconic leaders like Martin Luther King Jr., Gandhi, and Mother Teresa.

But peace can also be strong and active. It can be daring and bold. And it is something you can do every day. You can be a powerful peace-

Even your clothes can make a difference: these peacemakers promote positive change with their shirts.

maker right now. Because it is the "making" of peace that is important. No matter how big or small our actions are, they should move us and others toward a better, kinder, fairer, more loving place. A place of peace.

Peacemaking is being the positive change that has to happen right now. It means identifying a problem that you care about and working to make it better. It means taking risks and doing things that take courage. It is working with different people, not just the ones we like or who are easy to work with. It's crossing the barriers other people tell us we shouldn't cross because it is too difficult. It is loving other people—and ourselves—even when that feels really hard.

Peacemaking isn't always easy. If it were, we wouldn't have any problems in the world. But just because something isn't easy doesn't make it impossible. Or unimportant. Doing anything worthwhile—learning to swim or paint or multiply—takes practice, commitment, and starting with what you know.

Peacemaking is no exception. Peacemaking is not just a set of things you do, but a series of commitments that you make each and every day. As much as it seems that the big choices are what define us—where to go to school, which job to pursue, the families we build—these are actually outcomes of thousands of smaller, daily commitments we make about who we want to be in the world and which world we want to create. And you can and need to start making these daily commitments to peacemaking right now.

Because, despite what you may have been told, you do have the power to change the world. Not someone else. Not someday. But you. Right now.

Let's get started.

The Peacemaker Manifesto is a set of commitments to guide you on your journey. Think of it as an agreement you make with yourself and with the world.

Peacemaker Manifesto

I know the world can be a hard place. People are treated unfairly. People are hurting. This matters because people matter. All people. While I know I can't fix everything, I can make a choice to do something. I can choose to put peace first. And I commit to making this choice, every day.

To be a peacemaker, I make the following commitments:

COMMITMENT 1:
PUT PEACE FIRST, EVERY DAY.

A better world starts with a better me. Every day I will choose to do what is right, even if it is hard or uncomfortable. Every day I will choose to see the best in other people, even when they can't see it themselves. Every day I will choose to make myself, my community, and the world a better place for everyone. It is my choice. And I choose to be a peacemaker.

COMMITMENT 2:
RAISE MY HAND.

When I am confronted with an injustice or see a problem, I will raise my hand to do something. I won't wait for someone else to come along and solve the problem. I know the person who has to act is me.

COMMITMENT 3:
OPEN MY HEART.

I will act with kindness. I will work to really understand the needs and ideas of others, especially those I disagree with. I will share my own thoughts and opinions clearly and thoughtfully. I will try, in all that I do, to see the worth and dignity in everyone.

COMMITMENT 4:
TAKE A STAND.

I know that courage isn't about a lack of fear. It is being scared and still standing up, again and again, for what is right. It also means supporting others to stand up for themselves.

COMMITMENT 5:
BRING OTHERS ALONG.

I can do a lot by myself; I can do even more with others. I will use my brains and my heart to create opportunities for other people to be smart and courageous. Together, we will change the world.

COMMITMENT 6:
WORK WITH MY ENEMIES.

I will cross lines of difference to get things done. I will not let history, fear, or mistrust keep me from connecting with people who can help. I can find common cause on a few things without needing to agree on everything.

COMMITMENT 7:
KEEP TRYING.

I will own my mistakes and learn from them. I will apologize for the hurt I cause and learn how to be a more caring person. I will remind myself and everyone around me that we don't have to be perfect, we just have to keep trying to do what is right and just.

I refuse to accept the injustice in the world as it is. I will work with others to build a better world. For everyone. I will not back down. I choose to be a peacemaker.

COMMITMENT

1

PUT PEACE FIRST, EVERY DAY

A better world starts with a better me.
Every day I will choose to do what is right,
even if it is hard or uncomfortable. Every day
I will choose to see the best in other people,
even when they can't see it themselves.
Every day I will choose to make myself,
my community, and the world a better
place for everyone. It is my choice.
And I choose to be a peacemaker.

THE MOST IMPORTANT part of any journey isn't the destination or even the first step; it is the decision to go. That moment before you do anything, before you even say it out loud, when you decide that you will act. When faced with violence, hurt, bullying, and meanness, it makes sense that people choose to look away and do nothing, particularly if it doesn't affect them directly. This first commitment is to make a different choice: to see the problems in the world and to decide that you will do something about them. Even if you aren't yet sure what you will do. Even if you have no idea where to start.

The most important choices we make are the ones we make in our own hearts. Everything you do starts from this moment—the moment you decide that you want the world to be different, that *you* want to be different. Everything else flows from this choice. This first commitment is about getting started on your journey. Peacemaking is a choice. And it is a choice you will need to make again and again.

KATEBAH 15 YEARS OLD

It was heartbreaking after a second kid was shot in my neighborhood. We have this same assembly in the school. The same message was being related—come together, stop the violence. Yes, but we said that last time. How do we stop the violence? It isn't a formula. It's impossible. We need to do more than just stop the violence—we need to build community and we need to build peace. The way to become peacebuilders is to build community. —KATEBAH

OAKLAND, CALIFORNIA

> ## ❝ WE NEED TO DO MORE THAN JUST STOP THE VIOLENCE—WE NEED TO BUILD COMMUNITY AND WE NEED TO BUILD PEACE. ❞

Katebah and her family fled the poverty of her homeland in Yemen when she was just seven years old. Growing up in one of the poorest countries in the Middle East meant opportunities for education and jobs were few and far between. Arriving in the United States, everything felt different. Seeing snow for the first time and eating KitKats. Taking a yellow bus to school, tree-filled parks, and the rich cultural diversity of her new home in Oakland, California. All were welcoming examples of a new city, a new life, and a new opportunity.

But, as she soon discovered, violence and hurt were also part of this new American experience. Early in her first year of high school, a recent graduate was killed in a drive-by shooting by a rival gang looking for revenge. Her school held an assembly to mourn the loss. For Katebah and her classmates it was a sad story, but one they had all grown used to. This type of violence was a common occurrence. An hour later, everyone was back in their classrooms as if nothing had happened. Life went on.

A few months later, the brother of one of Katebah's classmates was killed in another drive-by shooting. He was five years old. He died in his father's arms before they could even call an ambulance for help. The school held another assembly.

As she sat in the same seat in the same auditorium hearing the same teachers' speeches, Katebah realized that not only was violence rampant in her community but a young person's death or injury wasn't even news anymore. It was just what happens. Another school assembly to announce another death and then back to normal. How had these tragedies been allowed to become normal?

Katebah knew it wasn't because people didn't care; it was because they had become numb and disconnected. A lack of community and connection meant that these deaths didn't seem real. They were statistics and news stories, not friends and neighbors. It was easy to see why no one chose to act. Where would someone even start? It was better not to even try.

In this moment, Katebah made a choice. She would not let this be normal. She would not keep returning to the auditorium with each new act of violence and then go back to class as if nothing had happened. Katebah would choose to do something. Even if, in that moment, she had absolutely no idea what that would be.

Katebah and her friends began talking about what could be done. They also talked with teachers they were close to. One issue that kept coming up was their city's lack of community, a commitment to shared sacrifice, a common purpose and connection. Katebah, her friends, and teachers started thinking about how they could find this sense of community. When they could not find it, they chose to create it themselves.

> ❋
>
> **KATEBAH WOULD CHOOSE TO DO SOMETHING. EVEN IF, IN THAT MOMENT, SHE HAD ABSOLUTELY NO IDEA WHAT THAT WOULD BE.**
>
> ❋

Each year the school organized a day of service in honor of Dr. Martin Luther King Jr.'s birthday in January and again at the end of March for Chavez Day, honoring the legacy of labor activist Cesar Chavez. To Katebah those days of service were a lot like the school assemblies: they were powerful for a moment—

everyone coming together with a shared purpose—but the next day it was back to the usual thing. What does that accomplish?

Katebah and her friends decided this year would be different. Starting with Dr. King's holiday and lasting the seventy-two days until Chavez Day they would organize a "fasting relay" to honor victims of violence—in all of its forms—and to create a shared sense of responsibility and connection. Every day a different student, community member, or teacher would fast—for twenty-four hours they would not eat any food and drink only water. The person fasting would wear a black armband so everyone in the school would be reminded of the cause. They would also write about the experience in a book to share with others. The fast would begin at noon and end at noon the next day with the whole group coming together to share about the fasting experience and pass the armband

Katebah (far right) and her friends swap armbands during their fasting relay.

on to the next person. In this way, they would all have a daily reminder and commitment to peace.

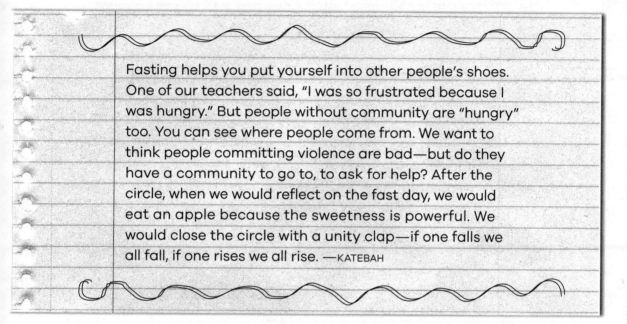

Fasting helps you put yourself into other people's shoes. One of our teachers said, "I was so frustrated because I was hungry." But people without community are "hungry" too. You can see where people come from. We want to think people committing violence are bad—but do they have a community to go to, to ask for help? After the circle, when we would reflect on the fast day, we would eat an apple because the sweetness is powerful. We would close the circle with a unity clap—if one falls we all fall, if one rises we all rise. —KATEBAH

To publicize their fast and to involve others, Katebah and her friends organized a march for peace and for community. Most marches in Oakland occur in response to a tragedy—a shooting, a death. This one was positive: a celebration of what they could accomplish together. More than three hundred people marched, coming from all over the city. They began by holding hands for a moment of silence and then burst out cheering and marching. During the following weeks, people from all over the country and the world learned of their fast through news stories and social media. Dozens and dozens joined their fasting in solidarity.

But not everyone was supportive. While the adults at the school encouraged Katebah's group, many adults in the community said they were wasting their time. This was just another plan that wouldn't accomplish anything. People suggested that Katebah and her classmates raise money instead to donate to violence prevention organizations. But for Katebah that missed the point: they weren't just trying to prevent violence; they wanted to build community. And sometimes the best way to build community is to stand alongside those who feel hurt, lost, or afraid.

The experience of fasting and sharing stories transformed the students and teachers who were involved. It changed the school too. Students at the school have always been required to do a service project; now the projects are required to have a peacemaking focus. While Katebah would love the fast to continue each year, she also knows that each class needs to find its own path, its own way of building community. That it is the commitment to change and taking that first step that matters most.

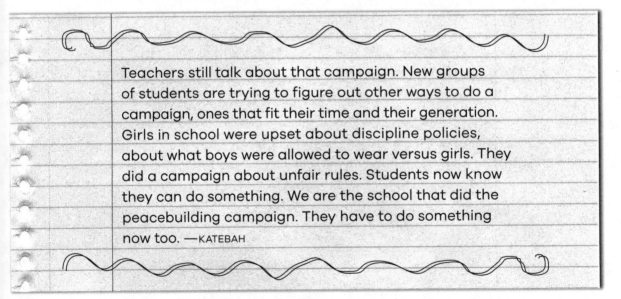

Teachers still talk about that campaign. New groups of students are trying to figure out other ways to do a campaign, ones that fit their time and their generation. Girls in school were upset about discipline policies, about what boys were allowed to wear versus girls. They did a campaign about unfair rules. Students now know they can do something. We are the school that did the peacebuilding campaign. They have to do something now too. —KATEBAH

A CLOSER LOOK

The problems of the world can feel overwhelming. It is impossible to fix them all. Images and stories from the news or even our own lives become too much, so we tune them out. There is more than enough to worry about without taking on other people's problems.

Katebah and her classmates made a different choice. Instead of looking away, they looked for the root of the problem and discovered a lack of community and connection. Rather than dismissing the victims who were shot as people who probably deserved it or someone else's problem, they understood the shootings as being important to everyone. And they chose to act by organizing and committing to a shared fast for several months. There were other important projects they could have worked on to make their school and city safer, fairer, and better. They chose one that helped build community and raise awareness.

But the key part of Katebah's story wasn't the fast or the rally or the shared commitment. It wasn't the local engagement or even the national news coverage. The most important moment happened in Katebah's school auditorium in that silent moment in her own heart when she decided she would act. When Katebah believed she could make a difference. When she believed she had to.

You can make that choice too.

★ START BY SAYING YES TO PUTTING PEACE FIRST.

Before you go out to change the world, you need to go into yourself, into your own heart. Make the commitment to make the world better and to make yourself better in the process. Say yes, even if you don't say it out loud or to anyone but yourself. Even if you aren't sure what you will do next. Start by saying yes: I commit to putting peace first, every day.

★ **SAY IT NOW.** There is no time to wait. The world needs you and it needs you now. There is too much to do for you not to get started. Something powerful happens in the moment you decide to make a difference. The world becomes different, even if it looks the same. Say it now: I choose to act.

★ **SAY IT AGAIN AND AGAIN.** Choosing to be a peacemaker isn't something that happens just once. It is a choice you make time and time again.

Committing to being a peacemaker isn't some magical moment where you suddenly become nice and patient and perfect all the time. There will be no bolt of lightning. It is more like planting a seed that you will need to care for consistently. You will need to protect it from harm. It might not grow the way you hope and might take longer than you'd like. But it all starts by putting the seed in the ground. By making the commitment to put peace first.

Advice from Katebah

If there is one issue that is affecting your community, the best way to go about solving it is to actually start making those connections, start talking to other people your age. When we start pooling our connections, it gives us so much more support, because every person you reach out to can only do so much. But when you all come together, everyone brings a little bit—maybe exactly what you need.

FROM COMMITMENT → TO ACTION

REFLECT:

Think back on the story and your ideas about this commitment.

1. What did you notice about Katebah's story? What do you most want to remember?

2. When was the moment she decided to act? What motivated her?

3. What aspect of Katebah's peacemaking work could you try in your own life?

TAKE STOCK:

Think about yourself, honestly, and what you know to be true right now.

1. When was a moment you made a big decision to try something new? What motivated you?

2. When was a time you made a sacrifice—big or small—for something you believe in?

3. Who are the people in your life who support you to be a better person or when you try something new?

TAKE ACTION:

Think about how you will apply the commitment to put peace first, every day. Below are three ideas to get you started.

1. Right now I will commit to putting peace first by trying one new peacemaking action.

2. Tomorrow I will tell one friend or family member about my new commitment.

3. Every day I will remind myself that the commitment to peacemaking has to be made again and again. I will write "I am a peacemaker" on a note and make sure it is the first thing I see every morning.

WHAT ELSE MIGHT YOU TRY?

COMMITMENT

2

RAISE MY HAND

*When I am confronted with an injustice
or see a problem, I will raise my hand
to do something. I won't wait for someone
else to come along and solve the problem.
I know the person who has to act is me.*

ONCE YOU HAVE decided to be a peacemaker, the next thing you need to do is act. Peacemaking requires a commitment to do something even—and especially—when it is uncomfortable or lonely. A lot of people don't act because they don't know what to do. Or they worry about standing out, or getting it wrong, or losing friends. Staying out of things is almost always the easier choice. Adults often say, "Mind your own business. Stay out of it. Just worry about yourself." From a young age, many of us are taught *not* to act.

But you cannot wait for someone else to step up. Choosing to be a peacemaker means that when you see a problem, *you* step up and you raise *your* hand and do what needs to be done. You are a peacemaker. It has to be you. It has to be now.

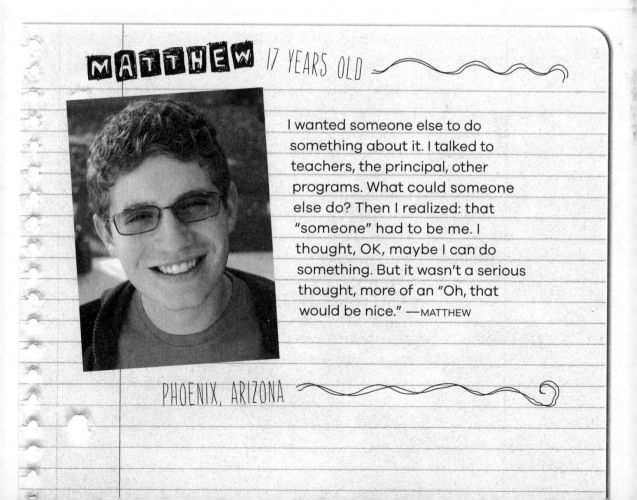

MATTHEW 17 YEARS OLD

I wanted someone else to do something about it. I talked to teachers, the principal, other programs. What could someone else do? Then I realized: that "someone" had to be me. I thought, OK, maybe I can do something. But it wasn't a serious thought, more of an "Oh, that would be nice." —MATTHEW

PHOENIX, ARIZONA

Matthew and his younger brother Josh could have been twins. Just nineteen months apart, they were incredibly close and complemented each other perfectly. Where Josh was confident and outspoken, Matthew was reflective and unsure. A soccer star, Josh was fearless in meeting people and making friends. Matthew felt timid on the outside: different, shy, insecure about his place in the world.

This began to change when they were both in middle school. Matthew had finally built a close group of friends and felt comfortable in his own skin. He got involved in theater and surrounded himself with people who really cared about him. Things went differently for Josh. Always more comfortable around girls than other boys, Josh found his circle of friends turning on him, excluding and taunting him, and tearing him down behind his back. A lot of the teasing happened online and through texts. The people he thought were his friends said mean things that they would never say to his face. His once confident spirit faded, and he became withdrawn and depressed.

> The kids who were bullying him were making fun of him online—friendly to his face, but would all go home and send text messages that they thought were innocent. "You suck." "You're stupid." Words when put in writing really magnified what he was already feeling about himself. That built up and snowballed and swallowed him. He didn't feel comfortable asking for help. Didn't want to admit that he was struggling, tried to save face. My parents and I noticed a shift in his behavior, his confidence. Even bigger, I realized it wasn't just a few bullies, but there is a culture that allows bullying to exist. —MATTHEW

Matthew kept waiting for someone—a caring adult with wisdom and experience—to step up and to step in. Someone better equipped to fix the torn relationships between his brother and friends. But his parents seemed as lost as he was about what to do. Teachers seemed mostly clueless about what was going on. After three months, while his brother continued to be terrorized, Matthew realized that the "someone" he was waiting for, the hero who would make everything better, was, in fact, himself. And while Matthew might not have had a ton of experience or education or power, he had something none of the adults around him had: he knew his brother and he knew what it was like to be in middle school and feel excluded.

---- ✳ ----

BUT HIS CONCERN FOR HIS BROTHER WAS BIGGER THAN HIS FEAR OF FAILURE.

---- ✳ ----

But how do you make middle school a safe place? Matthew realized that what schools usually do—punish "bad" kids, put up posters with positive sayings—doesn't really make a difference. He knew that if the school was going to change, it was going to be changed by the students themselves making different choices—to be kinder, friendlier, and more inclusive. The best way to help Josh was to help other students feel closer and connected. And the best way to do this was to get students talking to each other in a way that was safe and fun.

As excited as Matthew was by the idea, he was terrified of actually doing it. He was usually too scared to raise his hand in class, let alone speak in front of groups of students. He was anxious and worried about rejection. He was sure they wouldn't pay attention or—worse—would laugh at him. But Matthew's concern for his brother was bigger than his fear of failure.

Matthew shared his idea and worry with a teacher he trusted to see how he could get started. This teacher asked him, "What are you an expert at? What do you know?" Matthew thought about it for a few days. He had done a lot of theater and loved the way people came together when they did a play. Trust was built through games, working together, conversations, and activities that helped actors explore emotions and reactions. What if he could bring those same activities to his brother's classroom? A youth-led, fun, and safe workshop where middle school students could honestly share and connect might just spark kindness. It might help his brother feel less alone. Matthew didn't know anything about education or running programs, but as a young person himself, he knew how to get people talking and laughing.

He started by making a plan and relying on his own experiences and activities as a young person. He researched his favorite theater games and other ways to help students open up and share real feelings from their perspectives. Matthew spent three months carefully planning out

LEFT: Matthew presents his BeOne project to fellow students.

RIGHT: Matthew with peacemaker Brennan Lewis (left).

his workshop. It took a lot of thinking, trial and error, and practicing in front of the bathroom mirror. He also tried out ideas with friends he trusted and received a lot of feedback. He realized that what he thought was a good idea wasn't always. In fact, many of his initial ideas really bombed. But he also trusted his gut. He knew that he couldn't stand up in front of a class of middle school students unless he really believed in what he was saying.

Once the workshop was designed, he approached a few teachers he knew well and trusted. They served as advocates, setting up meetings with the administration and, eventually, giving Matthew a chance to present to all 120 teachers and administrators at his school. Talking in front of so many powerful adults was terrifying for Matthew, particularly because he knew he needed not only the teachers' approval but also their help to serve as volunteers for his youth-run lesson.

He introduced the idea, walked through each activity, what it would look like and how it would be

run. When he finished, the room was quiet. All of those grown-up eyes were staring at him. Then the room erupted into applause. He received a standing ovation. And permission to do a workshop in his brother's classroom two weeks later.

Josh didn't fully know what his brother was up to until the day Matthew presented to his class. Matthew was full of doubt as he looked out at the room full of seventh graders eyeing him with skepticism. Would they listen to him? More importantly, would they be willing to commit to being different? To being kinder and more accepting? While the workshop wasn't perfect—a few of the activities didn't work out as planned—the students loved it. They loved the chance to talk and connect and share through activities run by someone who was just a little older than them. Matthew saw the students open up in ways he didn't expect.

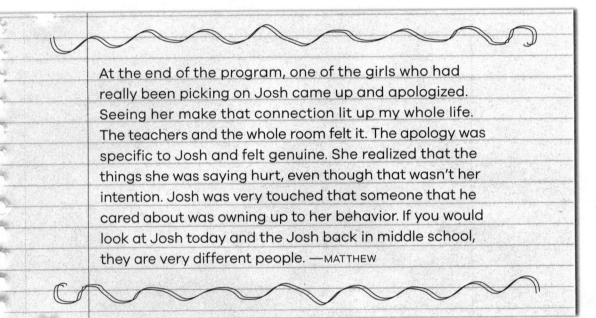

At the end of the program, one of the girls who had really been picking on Josh came up and apologized. Seeing her make that connection lit up my whole life. The teachers and the whole room felt it. The apology was specific to Josh and felt genuine. She realized that the things she was saying hurt, even though that wasn't her intention. Josh was very touched that someone that he cared about was owning up to her behavior. If you would look at Josh today and the Josh back in middle school, they are very different people. —MATTHEW

One of the teachers who had helped out with his first workshop invited Matthew to present to other grades. His program is now standard for all middle school students at his school. After each workshop, Matthew uses the feedback he receives to make the next one stronger. But his focus remains the same: offering youth-led activities that build a culture of kindness, student to student. Matthew has expanded his work to other schools around the country, inspiring other youth-led efforts to transform their schools.

All because Matthew realized that the "someone" who could make a difference was him.

A CLOSER LOOK

We all have moments like this. When we see something unfair happening that makes us angry. Sometimes it happens to someone we care about. Sometimes it happens to people we don't know, and still we are upset by it. Sometimes it happens to us. Matthew's brother was being bullied by a group of girls who were once his friends. He began to feel depressed and alone. Matthew kept waiting for someone else to do something about it. No one did. That doesn't mean that his parents or teachers didn't care. They did. But sometimes adults feel as helpless as young people do. Maybe even more so, since they have more years of experience with failure and powerlessness.

Matthew realized this issue was too important and his brother was too hurt not to act. Looking back at his choices, it might seem obvious that Matthew would step up, but he was terribly shy and anxious. He was the last person to make waves or challenge adults by arguing that their school was unsafe. It is easy to hear a story like Matthew's and think how simple it is to act. It was his brother, after all. And it all worked out great. He made a difference. Things got better for his brother. He created a program that is really helping kids all over the country. But of course that is not really how it happened. It wasn't easy for Matthew to act; he was terrified. He made mistakes. Some of his activities failed. As he took his program to other schools, adults didn't always take him seriously. He didn't just choose to raise his hand once to do something about a serious problem at his school. He chose to act again and again, even after something didn't work out.

What does it take to commit to raising your hand when you see a problem?

★ **REMEMBER THAT THE PERSON WHO NEEDS TO RAISE A HAND IS YOU.** You can't wait for someone else. This doesn't mean that you can't get help or talk to others. Sometimes raising your hand means finding a trusted friend or adult who can help. You don't need to spend all of your time tackling every one of the world's problems. Sometimes we have to focus on just one issue in order to make a difference. And you don't need to know exactly how you will help, only that you will. Sometimes simply raising your hand changes the world.

★ **YOU NEED TO DO SOMETHING NOW.** It is so easy to wait, as Matthew did, hoping that someone else will take care of it. So many terrible things have happened throughout history because "good" people stood around and said nothing. It makes sense. Why rock the boat? What if the person who is picking on another kid—a kid you don't really like much either—suddenly turns around and starts picking on you? Standing up can be risky. And sometimes this fear is so strong that you forget how powerful you really can be.

Sometimes choosing to act means deciding what *not* to do. When two of your friends are having an argument and you choose not to pick a side—that is choosing to be a peacemaker. When someone shares juicy gossip and you choose not to repeat it, you are being a peacemaker.

★ **YOU NEED TO CHOOSE TO SOLVE AN INJUSTICE THAT MATTERS.** The problem you tackle doesn't have to be big, but it does need to be meaningful. You don't need to organize a school assembly every time something bad happens. It can be as small as choosing to put only positive messages out on social media as an example to others. Your actions will inspire others. Commit to raising your hand to do something, and do it now.

Advice from Matthew

Dare to dream. Young people are put down for being dreamers—"You are naïve; in the real world things don't work that way." Tap into innate possibilities and optimism. Don't just dare to dream but put in the work and the time it takes to make dreams happen. Take the first step. You don't always need to know how everything is going to work out in this moment; but if you take the first step, things fall into place.

FROM COMMITMENT → TO ACTION

REFLECT:

Think back on the story and ideas about this commitment.

1. What did you notice about Matthew's story? What inspires you?

2. What fears did he have to overcome in order to act? How did he do this?

3. As you think about Matthew's peacemaking work, what ideas might you apply in your own life?

TAKE STOCK:

Think about yourself honestly, and what you know to be true right now.

1. When was a moment you took a risk to help someone else? What inspired you?

2. When was a moment you wanted to help someone but didn't? What stopped you?

3. Who are people in your life who inspire you to be your best self? What is it about them that inspires you?

TAKE ACTION:

Think about how you will apply the commitment to raise your hand in your everyday life. Below are three ideas to get you started.

1. Right now I will choose one issue or problem that I want to change to make the world a better place.

2. Tomorrow I will tell one friend or family member about what I want to change and ask for their support.

3. Each day I will look for one moment to help someone else. I will write down what I did every day and review what I wrote at the end of the month.

WHAT ELSE MIGHT YOU TRY?

COMMITMENT

3

OPEN MY HEART

I will act with kindness. I will work to really understand the needs and ideas of others, especially those I disagree with. I will share my own thoughts and opinions clearly and thoughtfully. I will try, in all that I do, to see the worth and dignity in everyone.

BEING A PEACEMAKER isn't just about working to make the world a better place. *How* you work to make the world a better place also matters. You need to be kind. You need to try to understand other people's points of view, especially people you disagree with. Once you've raised your hand to make a difference, you need to open your heart to the needs, ideas, and hurts of others.

Opening up your heart requires really listening to other people while communicating your own ideas clearly and with care. It means taking risks to connect with people who are different from you. It means truly understanding other people's perspectives while also understanding the effect of your own actions on others. Having an open heart means understanding what makes you angry yet being compassionate toward people who anger you. There is a lot wrong with the world. An open heart will help you understand why—and how to work with others to fix it.

DANIELLE 22 YEARS OLD

Growing up with cerebral palsy, having that disability, I have had a lot of obstacles that I've learned to overcome, whether it is verbal abuse by teachers— having them call me stupid or dumb—or just daily obstacles. It can get stressful for a young person to have the struggles that not everyone else has. On top of that, having the stress of going to school and having people point out all of those things. —DANIELLE

ST. JOSEPH, MINNESOTA

Danielle hated elementary school. Having cerebral palsy, which is a developmental and physical disability that affects muscle movements, posture, and fine motor skills like writing, made many daily tasks harder. She often had to use crutches to get around her crowded school. Her speech slurred slightly, meaning it took more time and effort for her to share an idea or answer a question. While she was able to keep up with her schoolwork, sometimes she needed a bit more time to understand a topic. Danielle only had a few friends at school. Most of her classmates wouldn't talk to her. They made fun of the way she walked. They called her ugly. In fourth grade, her teacher never called on her when her hand was raised. She even told her mother that teaching Danielle was a waste of time. She was too dumb to learn.

Hoping a smaller school might be a better fit, Danielle's parents enrolled her in a Catholic middle school. For the first time, Danielle was in a place that felt inclusive and welcoming and she had a teacher who took her seriously. She got the help she needed, made friends, and became involved in activities. But when she moved on to the public high school, even though she was excelling academically, Danielle again experienced cruelty and low expectations.

> **IT CAN GET STRESSFUL FOR A YOUNG PERSON TO HAVE THE STRUGGLES THAT NOT EVERYONE ELSE HAS.**

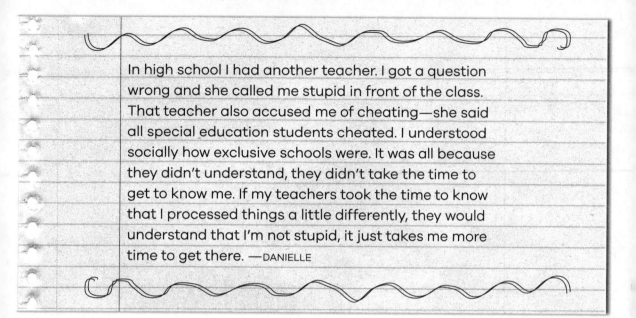

In high school I had another teacher. I got a question wrong and she called me stupid in front of the class. That teacher also accused me of cheating—she said all special education students cheated. I understood socially how exclusive schools were. It was all because they didn't understand, they didn't take the time to get to know me. If my teachers took the time to know that I processed things a little differently, they would understand that I'm not stupid, it just takes me more time to get there. —DANIELLE

One place where Danielle felt at home was with the Special Olympics. Special Olympics provides athletic and leadership opportunities to young people with disabilities. Given her passion and dedication, Danielle was invited to speak at forums across her state, encouraging audiences to see people with disabilities as equal and worthy. She wanted to bring the same spirit of inclusion and tolerance that she found through Special Olympics to her peers at school. As someone who bridged both worlds, she wanted to bring them together. She just didn't know how.

Danielle found her opportunity when she began college. She was always the first to speak up when people used mean words to dismiss people with disabilities. Other students took notice of her activism to make their college a more inclusive place. One particular student reached out to her. He had a brother with Down syndrome and got angry whenever people teased his brother or treated him like a baby. Would she be willing to meet and see how they could work together?

They talked for hours about how people on their college campus didn't have opportunities to interact with people with disabilities. Without these experiences, people were not able to broaden their understanding. And without this broader understanding, the mean behaviors that Danielle and her friend experienced would be repeated over and over again. For the most part, people weren't being purposefully cruel—they'd just never had an opportunity to meet and connect with people who were different.

> You can learn a lot from people. The people you meet are teachers, even if they are younger than you or they are older. I know it is a cliché: people have barriers out there that you are never going to experience. I have barriers that other people will never experience. Instead of telling people that they are not valued because of it, you need to respect it and let them teach you. This is how we learn. Not from a textbook. —DANIELLE

So they decided to start a club to raise awareness. Their goal was to educate other students about disabilities and share real stories of people who learn, walk, and live differently. They brought in speakers, including a family who had adopted five children from around the world, two of whom had disabilities. They hosted discussions afterward and tried their best to answer people's questions.

But bringing in speakers and hosting events didn't help people fully understand why life was so different for people with disabilities. To do

Danielle (third from left, center row) on the field with members of one of the teams she created.

that, the students needed to connect directly—to meet, to play, and to laugh—in ways that were safe and structured. So Danielle launched Unified Sports, a program that let students with and without disabilities play basketball together. Through her Special Olympics contacts, she knew twelve students with disabilities who wanted to play. This meant she needed twelve students without disabilities to join them. It was important to Danielle that the team feel balanced. She set up a booth outside the cafeteria to recruit potential players. In an hour she had more than one hundred people sign up.

With the success of the basketball team, she added other sports and created a mutual mentoring program that partnered two students—one with and one without disabilities—to spend time together, one-on-one. They also began a young athletes program where college students coached children with and without disabilities in activities together. Throughout these carefully organized and safe interactions Danielle noticed barriers were coming down. Again and again she heard from the young participants and her peers how different it was to connect and build friendships with actual people with disabilities rather than just reading about them. And from her friends with disabilities she heard how nice it was to be seen as a whole person, not just a statistic. It's easier to care about an issue when it's personal and real.

By partnering with her friend who didn't have a disability, Danielle modeled how people with and without disabilities could work together. It wasn't just college students helping kids with disabilities; it was people coming together to learn about each other, to ask questions, and to have fun. In three years their work grew from the initial twenty-four students playing basketball to more than two hundred doing all sorts of activities together. Open spots filled up within five minutes,

Danielle plays a game at a Unified Sports event.

and they had to limit people to being involved in only one program at a time.

Danielle also learned that change happens slowly and it takes time for people to form new opinions. You can't always see the daily impact. It can also be hard to stay motivated as a club leader when you also have to pay attention to budgets and organize meetings and van transportation. But when she shows up at an event and sees real connections happening, all those frustrations go away.

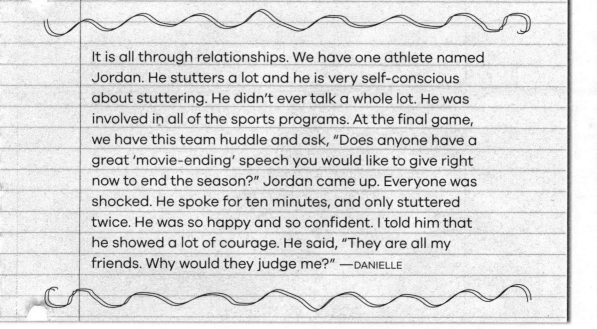

It is all through relationships. We have one athlete named Jordan. He stutters a lot and he is very self-conscious about stuttering. He didn't ever talk a whole lot. He was involved in all of the sports programs. At the final game, we have this team huddle and ask, "Does anyone have a great 'movie-ending' speech you would like to give right now to end the season?" Jordan came up. Everyone was shocked. He spoke for ten minutes, and only stuttered twice. He was so happy and so confident. I told him that he showed a lot of courage. He said, "They are all my friends. Why would they judge me?" —DANIELLE

A CLOSER LOOK

Danielle had no choice but to see the world differently from those around her. She walked and talked differently from the rest of her class. She often felt left out and angry. Rather than taking the time to understand her differences, her teachers dismissed her as too dumb to teach and her peers made fun of her. But Danielle knew that the issue wasn't that everyone around her was mean—they just didn't understand. Without opportunities to truly appreciate what life with a disability felt like, they just saw her as someone odd. But how do you help people appreciate something they cannot fully experience?

Understanding and caring about people who are different from us is a nice idea, but it's really hard to do, especially when it involves people we don't know or don't like. It requires seeing the world as another person sees it. It means learning about and valuing other people's opinions. Opening up your heart means taking on someone else's concerns as your own—even if there is nothing you can do to help except letting them know they aren't alone.

And letting people know they aren't alone can be more important than you might think. We all feel alone—different, misunderstood—at some point, and we think no one understands how we are feeling. Having people around us who really care about how we are doing, who listen to us, who understand who we really are, is such a great feeling. And it feels good to be able to do that for other people. So what stops us?

First, we often confuse understanding someone with agreeing with them. But you can care about people even if you don't see eye-to-eye with their beliefs or choices. In other words, it's possible to love someone but not always like what they are doing. This distinction is important because our judgments about other people can get in the way of caring about them. Set aside your own feelings to understand other people.

Second, it can be hard to understand other people's perspectives, especially if they are different from your own. While you might never truly understand what someone else is going through, it doesn't mean you shouldn't try. Take the time to understand how someone else's life is shaped.

Finally, when you feel misunderstood or hurt or alone, it is hard to open your heart. There are limits to how vulnerable we can be with others, particularly with people who hurt us. Opening up your heart to other people requires patience and care, but you can't ignore your own needs or feelings in your efforts to make other people comfortable. Just because you are working to understand someone else's feelings doesn't mean you should ignore your own. And just because you commit to being kind does not mean that you shouldn't also stand up for yourself and others.

So how do you start opening your heart?

★ **LISTEN. REALLY LISTEN.** As you are talking with someone—whether it is someone you know well or not—take a moment to really hear what they are saying. How do they seem as they are talking? Are they sad? Happy? Angry? Bored? Ask someone how they are doing and then really listen to the answer without trying to fix anything.

★ **SPEAK WITH CARE.** Listening is really important, but also pay attention to how you speak. How can you communicate your ideas clearly and kindly, even when you are disagreeing? Choose your words thoughtfully. Pay attention to how people react when you talk with them. Understand the effect of your words and actions on yourself and others.

★ **TAKE RISKS.** When you feel you are pretty good at listening and understanding the perspectives of people around you, take some risks. How can you care about and understand someone you don't know? How about someone you don't like? Compassion for friends is easy. Compassion for strangers and enemies is a lot harder.

And remember, just because you commit to understanding others does not mean that you shouldn't use your own voice and share your own thoughts. Compassion demands that we put ourselves in other people's shoes; just don't forget where you stand.

Advice from Danielle

People don't take the time to get to know each other. And if you can't put a face to the issue, it is hard to care about it. But if you want something to change, you have to do it, you have to start it. Show people how to do it with your actions, and then they will follow.

FROM COMMITMENT → TO ACTION

REFLECT:

Think back on the story and ideas about this commitment.

1. What did you notice about Danielle's story? What inspired you the most?

2. How did she work to understand people who were different from her? How did she help others do this too?

3. As you think about Danielle's peacemaking work, what strategies might you apply in your own life?

TAKE STOCK:

Think about yourself, honestly, and what you know to be true right now.

1. When was a time you tried to understand or appreciate someone you disagreed with? How did this work out?

2. Who is someone you have a really hard time with? What is it about this person that bothers you? Can you name one good thing about them?

3. Who are people in your life who are really kind to you and others? What is something about them that you admire? How could you try that too?

TAKE ACTION:

Think about how you will apply the commitment to open your heart in your everyday life. Below are three ideas to get you started.

1. Right now I will think of one person who drives me crazy and name three things I appreciate about them.

2. Tomorrow I will ask one person how they are doing and really stop to listen to their answer.

3. Every day I will find one person who looks like they are having a hard day and say something nice to them. I will write down that person's name and think about them before I go to bed.

WHAT ELSE MIGHT YOU TRY?

COMMITMENT

4

TAKE A STAND

*I know that courage isn't about a lack of fear.
It is being scared and still standing up,
again and again, for what is right. It also
means stepping aside so that others can
stand up for themselves.*

BEING A PEACEMAKER means you stand up for others. But while standing up and speaking out against an injustice looks like the brave and right choice, in the moment it can be terrifying. What if no one takes you seriously? What if it makes things worse? There can be consequences to taking a stand. You might get in trouble. You might lose friends. You might stand alone.

Being brave in the service of peace doesn't mean that you aren't scared. It doesn't mean that you aren't afraid about what will happen or that you might fail or look stupid. It is being worried about all of these things and standing up anyway. At its core, the commitment to taking a stand means you help others even when—especially when—there is risk involved. Not just when it is easy. This is what it means to be a peacemaker.

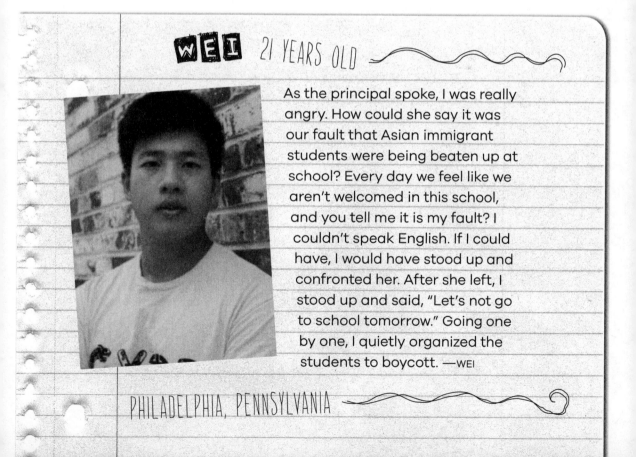

WEI 21 YEARS OLD

As the principal spoke, I was really angry. How could she say it was our fault that Asian immigrant students were being beaten up at school? Every day we feel like we aren't welcomed in this school, and you tell me it is my fault? I couldn't speak English. If I could have, I would have stood up and confronted her. After she left, I stood up and said, "Let's not go to school tomorrow." Going one by one, I quietly organized the students to boycott. —WEI

PHILADELPHIA, PENNSYLVANIA

Wei was born in a small village in Southeast China and moved to the United States with his family when he was fifteen. He had no idea what an American school would look like but expected it would be just like on TV—fancy, friendly, beautiful. But when he walked through the doors of his large Philadelphia high school, everything seemed broken and harsh. During his first month at school, two students punched him in the back of his head while he was at his locker. As he lay there on the floor, dizzy with pain, no one stopped to see if he was OK. The other students just stepped over him on their way to class.

A teacher brought Wei to the school security office to report what had happened. Wei was hopeful that someone at the school would help him, but instead they gave him a huge binder of student photographs and asked him to identify who had hit him. Because the attackers had come from behind, he hadn't seen their faces. They said there was nothing they could do to help.

Everyone acted like this incident was normal. Students get beaten up all the time, get over it. But Wei wouldn't get over it. Each day there were more fights. Most of the violence was directed at students like him: immigrants from Asia who spoke little English and therefore couldn't report it.

The adults at the school were just as bad. The lunch staff yelled. School security sat around joking, not intervening. They might say "stop" when there was a fight but not actually move from where they were. Unwilling to go to the cafeteria, where he might get attacked, and not allowed by his school to bring food in, Wei didn't eat lunch for his entire freshman year.

He hoped things would be better his sophomore year, but there were only more attacks against Asian immigrant students. In January, he was invited to a special meeting with the principal to discuss the problem. Wei was hopeful that, finally, someone was going to solve the problems that made school so difficult. But instead of trying to help, the principal brought all of the Asian students together to discipline them, saying that they weren't behaving well and that the attacks were their fault. If only they were more confident, she said, people wouldn't pick on them.

Wei was furious. It was bad enough that the school administration and staff weren't doing their jobs to keep them safe, but blaming the students themselves was the last straw. Wei convinced his fellow Asian immigrant students not to show up to school the next day. If the school refused to help them, then they wouldn't go.

The next day nearly every Asian student stayed home, demanding a meeting with the principal before they would return. At the meeting she blamed the safety issues on the district—they didn't provide enough security or cameras. When students stood to share their stories, she cut them off and denied everything

IF THE SCHOOL REFUSED TO HELP THEM, THEN THEY WOULDN'T GO.

Wei promoting his peacemaking efforts.

they said. The meeting ended without any progress. Wei and his fellow students returned to school the next day, feeling hopeless and frustrated.

But a few months later it came out that the principal had cheated on statewide tests and she was fired. The district promised a new principal and a safer school. For the first time since he had come to America, Wei hoped things could get better, both for him and for his fellow students.

They didn't. In fact things got worse. It was 8:30 on a chilly December morning when the first Asian student got beaten up in the middle of a class. The teacher just stood there. A few hours later, five Chinese students were beaten up in the hallway outside of the lunchroom. During lunch, two girls had trash cans thrown at them as they tried to run away. It seemed as if the whole school was falling apart. School administrators refused to call the police. They refused to call parents. They refused to intervene. By the end of the day, more than twenty-six students had been attacked; thirteen of them required hospital visits because their injuries were so bad. Hearing of the attacks, reporters flocked to the school, but the principal admitted only that there had been a fight or two, nothing serious.

Because he had organized them the year before, students looked to Wei to organize them again, to help them take a stand. Wei felt a tremendous amount of pressure, not just from his fellow students but from parents and community members too. Everyone was looking to Wei for a solution. What they didn't know was that he felt just as lost and helpless as they did. What would happen to him if he stood up to the school system? He might get expelled. He might get beat up again. He might get shot. Wei was terrified.

But he was also angry. He knew this had to end. He didn't want the students who came next to have to deal with this level of violence. He had to expose the situation to the public. No one else seemed to be standing up. Because he had done it before, it had to be him. His deep sense of anger and responsibility helped him overcome his fear. His plan was clear: if the school didn't value the Asian immigrant students, they would no longer show up for school.

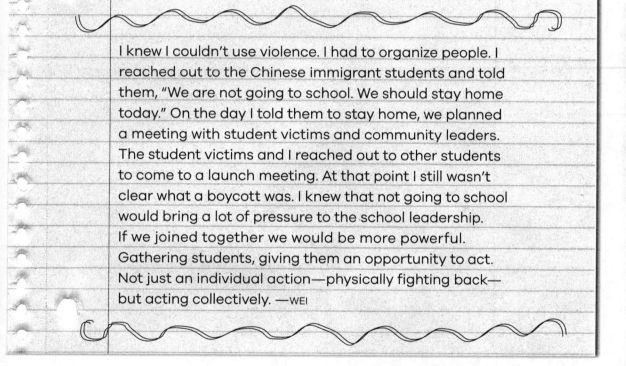

I knew I couldn't use violence. I had to organize people. I reached out to the Chinese immigrant students and told them, "We are not going to school. We should stay home today." On the day I told them to stay home, we planned a meeting with student victims and community leaders. The student victims and I reached out to other students to come to a launch meeting. At that point I still wasn't clear what a boycott was. I knew that not going to school would bring a lot of pressure to the school leadership. If we joined together we would be more powerful. Gathering students, giving them an opportunity to act. Not just an individual action—physically fighting back— but acting collectively. —WEI

Because the principal had lied to the press, Wei and other students held a press conference to explain what had really happened and to announce that they would not go back to school until there was a solution to the violence and their voices were truly heard. They would boycott until things changed. On the first day twenty students joined Wei's protest and stayed home from school. On the second day it was thirty-five. Then fifty. Then sixty-five. The school sent threatening letters warning parents that what the students were doing was illegal. But each day more and more students joined the boycott.

For Wei, organizing his fellow students wasn't easy. It took a lot of time to get everyone on the same page. And Wei had never done anything this big or public before. Everything had to be translated into four different languages. Wei knew the language barrier kept students from having a collective voice and from connecting with one another. He was now fielding calls from reporters, and community groups were asking him to speak to them. He had been taught to keep his head down and stay out of trouble. But he knew he had a role to play, to help students find a voice. Including himself.

Wei and other students lead a chant during the boycott.

On the fifth day of the boycott, Wei and his friends held a rally to demand a safe school. This time, more than three hundred people joined them—including members of the Latino, black, Asian, and white communities. All of them stood together with the students. Wei even reached out to and welcomed the same groups of students who had been attacking him and his friends. He knew that the attackers were victims of the same culture of violence that he was, and it went back generations.

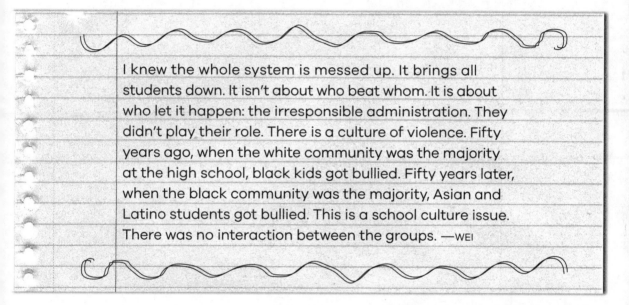

I knew the whole system is messed up. It brings all students down. It isn't about who beat whom. It is about who let it happen: the irresponsible administration. They didn't play their role. There is a culture of violence. Fifty years ago, when the white community was the majority at the high school, black kids got bullied. Fifty years later, when the black community was the majority, Asian and Latino students got bullied. This is a school culture issue. There was no interaction between the groups. —WEI

Wei and his classmates also filed a lawsuit with the U.S. Department of Justice, arguing that they had a fundamental right to be safe in their school. Wei's journal was the key piece of evidence; every day he had recorded what happened at school. Who got beat up. Who did it. Which adults knew about it and did nothing. He knew how important it was to tell the truth, even though he was scared of what could happen to him.

Six months later, they won the case. As part of the settlement the school finally committed to the real changes that Wei and the other students had demanded. Slowly the school improved—a new principal, sensitivity training for staff, a greater voice for students. It didn't transform overnight. But it did get better over time.

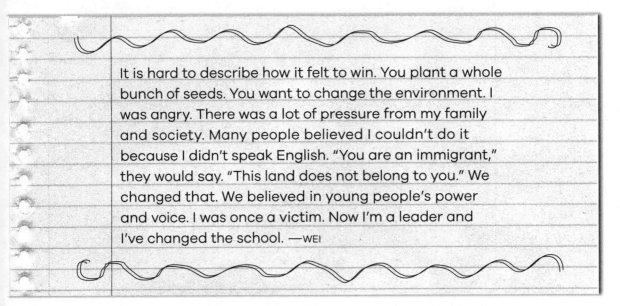

It is hard to describe how it felt to win. You plant a whole bunch of seeds. You want to change the environment. I was angry. There was a lot of pressure from my family and society. Many people believed I couldn't do it because I didn't speak English. "You are an immigrant," they would say. "This land does not belong to you." We changed that. We believed in young people's power and voice. I was once a victim. Now I'm a leader and I've changed the school. —WEI

A CLOSER LOOK

Imagine coming to a new school where very few students and none of the adults speak your language. Imagine another student attacks you in your first month while the adults whose job it is to keep you safe do nothing. Imagine this is happening to many other students—to most of your friends—and the principal blames you for not being "confident enough." Your parents want you to be quiet and just get along. You have never raised your voice, argued back, or even disagreed with an adult. You are angry but also scared about what might happen to you or your friends if you speak up. What would you do?

Wei chose to stand up for himself and others, but it didn't happen right away. It took months to find the courage and build the relationships. Wei faced a great deal of resistance—from his friends, who were scared of getting into trouble; from his parents, who thought he shouldn't make waves; and from a school that saw him as a problem. And he didn't do it alone. It was many students, acting together, that made it work.

We tend to think of courage as a single moment when someone takes a stand and changes the world. But as Wei shows in his story, courage can be made up of a lot of small moments of deciding to stand up for yourself, for others, or for an idea. Like so much about peacemaking, it is something you need to do again and again.

There are many ways to take a stand.

WHEN YOU STAND UP FOR YOURSELF. This might sound selfish, but when you stand up for your own needs you send a message that no one deserves to be treated badly. Wei was scared about what might happen to him at school every day. He worried about his safety. When he stood up and said he was no longer going to be part of a school that treated him so poorly, Wei was inviting others to take a stand along with him.

WHEN YOU STAND UP FOR AN IDEA. Wei didn't just stand up for himself and his fellow students. He stood up for a belief: that students have a right to feel safe at school—all students, including ones who were making his life miserable. When you stand up for an idea that is bigger than your own experience, you allow others to stand alongside you.

WHEN YOU STAND UP FOR OTHERS. Too often people get used to being treated a certain way. "That's just how it is," they say. "I can't do anything about it." Standing up when other people are being treated unfairly is powerful. Wei could have survived another year until he graduated and left the problem for someone else to figure out. But he knew that there would be more students who felt the way he did. He cared about them. He wanted the world to be different for them.

WHEN YOU HELP OTHERS TO STAND UP FOR THEMSELVES. Sometimes taking a stand means creating space for other people's bravery, supporting others to stand up for themselves. We need to be careful about how we act so as not to make others feel powerless. There are times when the brave thing to do is to simply ask, "How can I help?" and "What do you need?" Never do for others what they should do for themselves.

So how can you be courageous in your everyday life?

★ **FIRST, IT IS IMPORTANT TO REMEMBER THAT COURAGE LOOKS DIFFERENT FOR ALL OF US.** If you are shy, simply raising your hand and asking why a situation is the way it is can be a really brave act. If you are comfortable speaking out, holding back so someone else can be a leader takes a great deal of courage. You cannot measure your own courageousness by any standard but your own. What is easy for you might be very hard for someone else.

★ **SECOND, TAKE A FEW SMALL RISKS.** Start with understanding what keeps you from speaking up in unfair moments—for yourself or for others—and take a few calculated risks. If you have a family member who says unkind things about a group of people and you never say anything, practice what you might say the next time you hear him sounding off. Sit next to someone eating alone at lunch, even if you are worried about what others might think. For a week, say hello to everyone you pass on the street. If you have never run a club meeting, volunteer to run the next one. The idea is not to be perfect but to try taking risks. Courage is like any other skill or muscle in your body—the more you use it the stronger it gets.

★ **FINALLY, BE PATIENT WITH YOURSELF.** As you work to become braver, pay attention to the moments when you don't stand up. Why do you hang back? What is it about certain situations that makes it harder to be brave than others? Maybe it's harder around your friends than strangers because you are worried about what they might think. Or maybe it's the other way around—you are very comfortable speaking out with your friends but not with people you don't know. Don't beat yourself up for missed opportunities—this isn't a courage competition—but do pay attention and learn about what holds you back and what helps you stand up.

Another opportunity to take a stand for something you believe in is just around the corner.

Advice from Wei

Speak up for yourself and stand up for the right things you believe in. The whole environment we grow up in can be challenging. It will still be challenging until you take action to change that. To accept the challenge is really important because it is helping us to grow up. I always use this quote: "We have the power to make change."

FROM COMMITMENT → TO ACTION

REFLECT:

Think back on the story and ideas about this commitment.

1. What did you notice about Wei's story? What happened to him that bothered you the most?

2. In what ways was Wei courageous? How did he help others to be brave?

3. As you think about Wei's peacemaking work, how might you take risks in your own life?

TAKE STOCK:

Think about yourself, honestly, and what you know to be true right now.

1. When was a time you took a stand for someone else or an idea—big or small? What motivated you to get involved?

2. When was there a moment something bad happened and you didn't speak up? Why?

3. Being brave means different things to different people at different times. What risks might you be willing to take to help someone else or for a cause you believe in?

TAKE ACTION:

Think about how you will apply the commitment to take a stand in your everyday life. Below are three ideas to get you started.

1. Right now I will think of one way I can stand up for another person or an idea.

2. Tomorrow I will speak up at least once to support someone, perhaps someone I don't know or like.

3. Every day I will notice when someone else takes a risk on behalf of peace and I will appreciate them.

WHAT ELSE MIGHT YOU TRY?

COMMITMENT

BRING OTHERS ALONG

I can do a lot by myself; I can do even more with others. I will use my brains and my heart to create opportunities for other people to be smart and courageous. Together, we will change the world.

WE TEND TO think that positive change happens with amazing individuals in specific moments. In fact, all real and lasting change occurs when groups of people come together. A team can use its different skills, ideas, and relationships to help solve problems. It can provide support and comfort when times are tough, and share in celebrating during moments of success. Individual leaders certainly matter. Great teams matter more.

As a peacemaker, you can do a lot by yourself, but you will do even more with others. The world doesn't need superheroes or martyrs. Bringing others along means creating opportunities for other people to be smart and courageous. As a peacemaker, you commit to working with other people who have skills and relationships that you do not have, to make the work stronger and longer lasting. People who commit to organizing others are indispensable for creating positive change.

JEREMIAH 18 YEARS OLD

Most people don't wake up and say, I'm going to be bullied today. So why does it happen? I saw what experts say: most bullies just want attention and validation and want to feel good about themselves. How can I give people these things, to validate them? Compliments would be good. And since I couldn't go door to door to people's houses to deliver compliments, I figured Twitter would be the best way.

—JEREMIAH

IOWA CITY, IOWA

Jeremiah considered himself an ordinary kid. He attended a large sub-urban high school in Iowa where he had a close group of friends that went largely unnoticed at the school. He did track and field but wasn't a superstar. He was involved in a few clubs—Disney Club (where they watched Disney movies), volunteering club, Spanish club, and speech and debate—but wasn't a leader in any of them. He was funny and out-going with those close to him, but shy and quiet with everyone else. He wasn't an outcast or a social butterfly.

As at many schools, the administrators at Jeremiah's were worried about student bullying. And as at many other schools, their answer was to pull all of the students into the auditorium to hear a speaker discuss why bullying was bad and warn students that they shouldn't bully or let others be bullied. While he sat in the auditorium listening to the speaker, Jeremiah thought to himself, *OK. Everyone knew that already. But what should we actually do about it?*

Jeremiah had never been bullied in his life. People might say neg-ative things to him from time to time, but he never felt threatened or intimidated by other students. While the issue wasn't personal to him, he did notice its effects on his school community, particu-larly the cruel things people would say about each other online. His classmates felt freer to be mean when they were writing on screens—even meaner than when face-to-face. Even though the bullying was happening online, it also showed up every day in the hallways. The cumulative effects of these small cruelties added up to an unkind school atmosphere.

Jeremiah knew people didn't wake up and choose to be victimized that day. Nobody wants to be bullied. And most people who pick on oth-ers are just trying to feel better about themselves, looking for attention and validation. If bullies ultimately want to feel good about themselves,

> **" MOST BULLIES JUST WANT ATTENTION AND VALIDATION AND WANT TO FEEL GOOD ABOUT THEMSELVES. "**

how could this need be met in positive ways? How could he replace the negative and cruel comments circulating online and in the hallways with something positive and uplifting?

Jeremiah's answer was simple: compliments. Sending positive messages to lift people up, underscore their goodness, and share the awesomeness that he knew existed within everyone. And because social media was the place where the worst comments were being made, he would use that same platform. He created a Twitter handle called @WestHighBros to spread positive energy and compliments to his fellow students.

But Jeremiah knew that they couldn't be just any type of compliments. First, each compliment had to be sincere. The feelings behind the compliment had to be real. If they weren't, then it wouldn't be meaningful. Second, it had to be personal and specific. Otherwise it would just be generic fluff like those inspirational posters in his guidance counselor's office ("Hang in there!" "You can soar like an eagle!"). A powerful compliment had to feel honest and meaningful to the person receiving it.

The problem was Jeremiah didn't know most of the two thousand students at his school. His school was divided into many different groups and competing social networks. He couldn't do this alone; there was just no way for him to reach everyone. To share genuine and personal compliments throughout the school he needed to find other people to help him. And he had to reach outside his own circle of friends, to people he didn't know.

Jeremiah made a list of the various clubs and groups in his school—chess club, French club, wrestling, football, et cetera—and identified each group's leaders. He approached each person directly to see if they might be interested in helping him. Jeremiah had to make sure that the leaders he talked to shared his vision for positive social media messages and that they were people he could trust and count on. That didn't mean they were his friends; in fact, in most cases he barely knew them.

He started by looking at what they tweeted from their own accounts. Were they connected to others? What words did they share? Were they kind? Were they living a life that felt positive and inclusive? Were their messages genuine? Jeremiah didn't just want to find students who would reach as many people as possible; he wanted partners who would model caring and kindness in everything they did and spread the message far and wide.

---— ✳ ——---

WORKING TOGETHER THEY NOT ONLY COVERED THE WHOLE SCHOOL BUT HELPED EACH OTHER GET BETTER AT PUTTING FORTH GENUINE AND PERSONAL COMPLIMENTS.

---— ✳ ——---

In issuing the invitation, Jeremiah asked two questions: "Would you like to join @WestHighBros to spread positivity throughout the school?" If the answer was yes, he asked, "Would you try tweeting a compliment to the person you dislike the most?" If this challenge intrigued them and they wrote a genuine and specific compliment, Jeremiah knew he had found a partner. If not, he thanked them for their time.

Jeremiah recruited ten partners to ensure that @WestHighBros would spread throughout the school with sincere and personal compliments. Taking turns, they sent out positive tweets throughout the day, calling out the great things that might get overlooked (*Saw @pineappl3s sacrifice his shoe to get the basketball of a little boy unstuck today. Not all heroes wear a cape.*) and the successes of their school (*Congrats to the boys football team and the girls volleyball team on their huge successes this week!*). Working together, they not only covered the whole school but helped each other get better at putting forth genuine and personal compliments.

Jeremiah (front) at a peacemaking event with siblings and actors Ehsan (left), Yara (center), and Sayeed Shahidi (right).

Their positivity became contagious. After a few months, students outside of the original small group of tweeters were sharing compliments and positive messages, online and off. By the end of the school year, bullying had decreased dramatically at the school. @WestHighBros soon had thousands of followers, not just at the school but from all over the world as students in other schools started creating positive Twitter accounts for their schools.

Not everyone liked @WestHighBros. Because there were several

Jeremiah (center) with fellow peacemakers.

news stories about the project, some people thought Jeremiah and his team were just doing it for the attention. One person tried to hack the account; another kept making fun of the tweets with parodies. Jeremiah even received threatening notes on his locker. He sometimes doubted himself—maybe there was a reason people were saying all of these mean things about him. But each time that happened, another student would tell him what a difference @WestHighBros had made in their life.

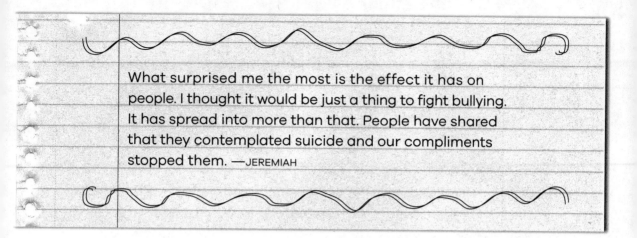

What surprised me the most is the effect it has on people. I thought it would be just a thing to fight bullying. It has spread into more than that. People have shared that they contemplated suicide and our compliments stopped them. —JEREMIAH

When Jeremiah leaves for college, he plans to hand over the leadership to a new group of students. He can't give authentic and personal compliments when he is no longer there. He can also imagine a time when the account will be shut down because it isn't needed. When people will have the spirit of @WestHighBros within themselves.

A CLOSER LOOK

You could look at Jeremiah's story and see an incredible leader. He saw a problem. He came up with a cool idea and created a program that made his school kinder and safer. He faced criticism and doubters but did it anyway. He made a powerful difference. This is the story usually told about how problems get solved: One brave leader steps forward with an answer and saves the day.

There is another way to understand this story. Jeremiah couldn't solve the problem on his own. All he had was an idea. He needed other leaders and their social groups to be successful. Other students had the key relationships and did much of the work. Not only did they make his idea better, they actually made it possible. Jeremiah was key in getting the project off the ground. But so were the others who joined him to make @WestHighBros work.

When making the world a better place, there is a lot you can do by yourself. You can make quick decisions and speak with one voice. You can get things done without worrying about whether others agree with you. You can inspire people through your example. You can move fast to respond to opportunities or crises.

But you can do even more with others. You can make better decisions with more perspectives and input. You can speak with a collective voice, showing the power of many, not just the opinion of one person. Others can share the work and offer different talents and points of view. It is more effective, in the long run, to have partners sharing the work. Jeremiah's project is a great example of what happens when you bring others along in your peacemaking efforts.

But just because something is more effective doesn't mean it is easier. Working in groups can be hard. It requires sharing decision making and giving up some control. There will be conflict and disagreements. People sometimes disappoint—they miss meetings or deadlines, or they may not seem as committed as you. It can take forever to do simple things when you bring others along with you. In those moments, it's key to remember that being a peacemaker means creating opportunities for other people to be smart and courageous. But how?

★ **FIRST, START WITH WHOM YOU KNOW.** Who are two or three people you admire, trust, or can learn from? Reach out to them to share your ideas or worries. What do they think? What do they care about? How can they help? Remember that the best ideas are often created collaboratively.

★ **SECOND, DEFINE CLEAR AND MEANINGFUL OPPORTUNITIES.** Be specific about what you are inviting people to do. What will get people excited? People join groups for different reasons, and they are good at different things and will take on different roles. Mostly people want to feel that they are being helpful and they have a say over what they do. Create opportunities for others to feel useful, to use their skills in ways that are meaningful to them. Embrace differences among the team. In creating @WestHighBros, Jeremiah made sure a common goal was set, but that everyone could reach it in their own way. He used people's natural differences to create success.

★ **FINALLY, BE PATIENT, BOTH WITH YOUR TEAM AND WITH YOURSELF.** Bringing people along can be hard. It will take time to get everyone on the same page. There will be disagreements. At each of these moments your commitment to being a peacemaker will be tested. When this happens, take a step back to remind yourself, and others, why you are doing this work.

Remember this wise proverb: If you want to go fast, go alone. If you want to go far, go together.

Advice from Jeremiah

Instead of saying, "I'm going to build the perfect wall," say, "I'm going to lay the perfect brick." Peacemaking isn't the goal, it is the step; it is every single step.

FROM COMMITMENT → TO ACTION

REFLECT:

Think back on the story and ideas about this commitment.

1. What did you notice about Jeremiah's story? What felt most creative?

2. How did Jeremiah involve other people? What seemed key to getting others to help?

3. As you think about Jeremiah's peacemaking work, how might you get others to join you?

TAKE STOCK:

Think about yourself, honestly, and what you know to be true right now.

1. What is easy for you about working with other people? What do you enjoy most?

2. What is hardest for you about working with other people? What drives you crazy?

3. When are moments you most like working with others? When do you like working alone? Why?

TAKE ACTION:

Think about how you will apply the commitment to bring others along in your everyday life. Below are three ideas to get you started.

1. Right now I will think of one person I want to work with to make the world a better place.

2. Tomorrow I will reach out to two people to ask them how they want to make our community stronger, safer, better.

3. Every day I will pay an honest and genuine compliment to one new person and record their reaction.

WHAT ELSE MIGHT YOU TRY?

COMMITMENT

WORK WITH MY ENEMIES

I will cross lines of difference to get things done. I will not let history, fear, or mistrust keep me from connecting with people who can help. I can find common cause on a few things without needing to agree on everything.

BEING A PEACEMAKER means not only working with people you like but with people who can help you create the change you want to see. Many times, these are not your friends or even people you get along with. Effective and lasting change is made across lines of difference and disagreement. This isn't about becoming best friends with someone you don't like; it's about finding a common cause to work on in the name of justice.

Working with your enemies (or at least those people who seem like they are) requires finding good and possibility in unlikely places. Very often the most useful partnerships end up being with those who you are actively fighting against. Because if you can change the minds of people who disagree with you, then anything is possible. Understanding your friends and their needs is easy. Understanding your enemies is part of peacemaking.

BABATUNDE *18 YEARS OLD*

I was interning at a radio station, heading home from work, with my hand out the window, driving the speed limit when the police stopped me. They assumed I had seen them following me and had thrown drugs out the window to avoid getting caught. In actuality, I didn't realize they were behind me until they pulled us over. They put me on the curb and wanted to do a search. I said, "I don't consent to a search."

BALTIMORE, MARYLAND

"Who do you think you are?" they yelled. "We will beat the crap out of you. Don't let us have to beat the crap out of you." I was humiliated. I was with my friend. It was the afternoon. People were out. A friend from high school drove by and saw me like that. It was really embarrassing, not having control. The police tore the car apart. As they were letting us go they shouted, "Just to let you know: if you were in West Baltimore we would have beat the crap out of you. But we'll see you again." That was my first terrible interaction with the police. I knew on a theoretical level it was bad, but now I realized it is a rite of passage for a black person in Baltimore. —BABATUNDE

Babatunde was a nerdy kid who loved football, chess, Marvel comic books, and science fiction. He had a tight group of friends but didn't socialize a lot out of school. He was short for his age and preferred to blend in rather than to stand out. He was just as close to his religious father, who pushed him to do well in school and sports, as he was to his more laid-back mother, who encouraged his creative side.

When he was fifteen, Babatunde joined an after-school program because he needed community service hours for school. Plus, it was conveniently located across the street from his home. The program taught video production skills and helped young people tell stories that mattered to them. Most of the videos focused on problems the young people noticed around Baltimore. One of the videos told the story of a kid who went downtown to skateboard and was knocked off his board by a police officer. The officer was fired for his behavior. The kid was white. For Babatunde and his friends, this was a revelation: This type of treatment by the police happened to them—black kids from Baltimore—all the time and no one ever got fired.

What started off as required community service became a passion to make a difference as the police harassed more of his friends. Then Babatunde had his own experience. Driving home from his summer internship, he was stopped for suspicion of possessing drugs, searched, roughed up, and released with a threat.

For many of his peers, the response to these interactions with the police was anger, mistrust, and fear. That was true for Babatunde too; but he was also curious:

> I guess I didn't really understand. When I see videos of officers treating people wrong, I think, What is going through this man's head? Racism? Bad day? Stress? As a young person I was curious about what was the cause. Policies? Quotas? —BABATUNDE

Babatunde genuinely wanted to understand why the dynamic between the police and young black people in his community was so dangerous. He wanted to understand the perspective and experiences of the cops he and his friends were so afraid of. His after-school coordinator invited a group of officers to speak with Babatunde and his peers. As they sat together in a circle, police officers and young people, Babatunde was surprised to hear the officers speak so openly about racism and crime and their own experiences in their jobs. He realized that, like him, they were mistrustful and worried about the relationship between themselves and the communities where they served. Everyone left with a better understanding and appreciation of each other's experiences.

Since that initial conversation went so well, the police officers invited Babatunde and his team from the video production program to run a larger workshop in which young people and officers could have candid conversations. Although Babatunde didn't have much hope that it would make a difference, that summer he organized a pilot program for half a dozen police officers, most of whom were new to the force and seemed open to honest, sometimes tough, conversations with young people. "Why do young people commit crimes?" "What do officers do that angers young people?" "What do you do when you see another officer step out of line?" Several of them admitted to seeing fellow officers do things that bothered them but believed they had to protect one another.

Babatunde and his team met with the officers for two hours every week for three months and really got to know them. Soon the officers weren't just cops, they were people with whom Babatunde had real and honest conversations.

Even though the conversations went well, deciding to work with police offers was a risky decision for Babatunde.

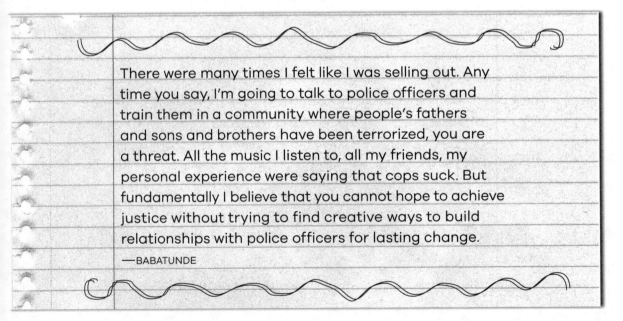

There were many times I felt like I was selling out. Any time you say, I'm going to talk to police officers and train them in a community where people's fathers and sons and brothers have been terrorized, you are a threat. All the music I listen to, all my friends, my personal experience were saying that cops suck. But fundamentally I believe that you cannot hope to achieve justice without trying to find creative ways to build relationships with police officers for lasting change.

—BABATUNDE

Babatunde felt confident and wanted to do more. He wanted to see how he and his team could transform the culture of policing throughout Baltimore. Working with other young people, he came up with a curriculum for monthly trainings based on the two areas the officers thought were most important: educating police officers

Babatunde during one of his workshops with Baltimore City police officers.

about what the law allowed them to do (and not to do) and being able to relate better with young people. Based on those two ideas, he created a series of videos that featured young people and other community members sharing their experiences with the police. When was the last time you got pulled over or saw someone in your family have a negative interaction with the police? How did it feel and how did it affect your feelings about the police? Babatunde was excited to share the stories of people who were passionate about creating change directly with the police. The police department gave him permission to train large groups of officers throughout the city.

The first three trainings Babatunde led were terrible. Unlike the small group of rookie officers his team got to know so well over the summer, this larger group had more veteran officers who were often dismissive. There were shouting matches—officers telling Babatunde and his friends that they didn't know what really went on in the world. They showed way too many videos. It wasn't interactive. The officers were bored. In a room of seventy police officers, the last two rows often fell asleep.

Babatunde and his team regrouped. Rather than showing videos, they designed role-playing games in which officers were challenged to participate in in-depth scenarios. What is it like being a single mother raising three boys and your son hasn't come home all night? What if you are a principal and one of your best students is suspected of selling drugs at the school? What if you are the student selling drugs? The young people played the cops. The officers became active participants in the workshops by putting themselves in other people's shoes. The young people had to do the same. Babatunde realized he had something really powerful.

But he still wondered if he was really having an impact. Many of the officers conveyed a sense of entitlement: "We don't have to listen to you. Who are you to teach us?"

After almost every workshop, though, a handful of police officers shared something different: "I'm glad you came. This is important. I've been trying to say this to my colleagues. Glad young people are taking initiative." Each workshop meant three hours of feeling tense and stressed—worrying whether it was even working. But when they talked to these supportive police officers afterward, they knew they were having an impact.

Babatunde and his team trained hundreds of police officers—two-thirds of the Baltimore Police Department—three hours a month for twelve months. While it wasn't always easy, he and his team built productive relationships with the officers by helping everyone understand each other's experiences. They began to break down significant barriers of suspicion, anger, and hurt.

Babatunde realized it was just a start, that you cannot change generations of mistrust and frustration in a single year. But sometimes, by working with those you have been fighting against, a new relationship can blossom.

A CLOSER LOOK

Babatunde had every reason to mistrust the police. All of his life he had heard stories of aggressive police misconduct and violence, and he witnessed the harassment himself. His own humiliating experience of being stopped and threatened in the middle of the day while his friend's car was torn up in a search fueled his anger. Yet he was also curious: Why was the relationship between black people and the police the way it was? And who says it has to be this way? He decided to find out.

This was not an easy choice. In deciding to train the police, Babatunde put himself at risk. People in his neighborhood, even his friends, were skeptical about his motives and strategy. Some viewed his work as an act of betrayal. How could he work with the enemy? But the police department took a risk too, by inviting a seventeen-year-old to train its officers.

When there is a struggle or conflict going on, people expect you to choose sides and to show your commitment to your cause and your people. Instead Babatunde chose to look for a solution in an unlikely place—the very group he was angry with. He was committed to working for change, even though it meant risking friendships and his reputation. A decision like this isn't easy. It can make you feel lonely and confused. It can also lead to greater understanding and new relationships.

Babatunde didn't learn to love the police through his workshops, although he did come to understand and appreciate a few individual officers and the tough role of policing. Not all of the officers were prepared to listen to the young people. But some did. And these two groups with a strained and painful history figured out how to work together.

Being a peacemaker means not only working with people you like or agree with. It also means working with those who can best help you create the change you want to see. The good news is it's possible to find common cause on a few things without agreeing about everything. Babatunde could partner with the police officers to help them understand the experiences of young black people, and they could help young black people understand what it was like to be a police officer. They both wanted better relationships, and by focusing on what they shared, it opened up the possibility of joining together on something they both cared about.

It is hard enough to work with your friends; how do you do this work with your enemies?

★ **START BY ASKING WHO.** Who are some of the people or groups that you feel are standing in your way? Maybe someone in your school is unkind to you or your friends. Maybe you want to increase the role students play in making policies at your school but the teachers seem against it. Perhaps you have an uncle who says things you find offensive or a grandparent who has different views about the world. Or maybe there is a company that is dumping trash in a place where you think they shouldn't. Identify who is standing in your way.

★ **ONCE YOU FIND THE PEOPLE, THEN FIND THEIR HUMANITY BY ASKING WHY.** Why do they feel the way they do? What do they care about? Why is this important? Get to know them and, more importantly, get to know their point of view. Babatunde and his friends found two police officers they could talk to in order to see their point of view. This helped them understand the challenges they would have to overcome to train police officers.

★ **EXPLORE.** What do you have in common? What do you share? What do you both care about? Babatunde found there were officers, just like him and his friends, who wanted a safer community and better relationships. Focus on one thing you have in common and build from there.

★ **ACT.** Start with something small to test how it will be to work together and to build trust. What is a simple activity you can do together? Perhaps your teachers might be open to an easy project that students could lead. See how it goes and then see how it can grow. What could you do next?

★ **FINALLY, BE REALISTIC AND BE SAFE.** Working with people who see the world differently from you can be hard and messy. It can also be dangerous. People might take advantage of your kindness or use your work together to distract from deeper problems and injustices. The police, for example, might promote their partnership with Babatunde to avoid making other reforms or tackling other problems. There might be people or groups so strongly against your work that they won't even engage. But that doesn't mean you shouldn't seek opportunities to cross lines of difference and search for common humanity, even in inhumane places. As Bishop Desmond Tutu, who helped lead a peaceful revolution in South Africa, noted, "If you want peace, you don't talk to your friends. You talk to your enemies."

Advice from Babatunde

I think that it is the system that is doomed to fail, not the individuals. You could get a lot of hate and anger if you think about individuals as terrible people. It makes me realize that you need to look at the institution that is being ineffective, not the people in them.

FROM COMMITMENT → TO ACTION

REFLECT:

Think back on the story and ideas about this commitment.

1. What did you notice about Babatunde's story? What moment felt bravest to you?

2. How did Babatunde connect with the police? What risks were involved in this partnership?

3. What are the limits of working with your enemy? In which situations could it be helpful? When might it be dangerous, to you or the cause you believe in?

TAKE STOCK:

Think about yourself, honestly, and what you know to be true right now.

1. When was a time that you reached out to work with someone different or difficult? How did it go?

2. What people or groups drive you crazy? Why do you think you find them so frustrating?

3. What might you be willing to give up to ensure the success of your peacemaking work? What would you never compromise on?

TAKE ACTION:

Think about how you will apply the commitment to work with your enemies in your everyday life. Below are three ideas to get you started.

1. Right now I will think of one person I disagree with whose help could make the world a better place.

2. Tomorrow I will reach out and learn one thing I have in common with a person or group I disagree with.

3. Every day I will read something written by a person or group that sees the world differently from me and try to understand one thing that is important to them.

WHAT ELSE MIGHT YOU TRY?

COMMITMENT

7

KEEP TRYING

I will own my mistakes and learn from them.
I will apologize for the hurt I cause and
learn how to be a more caring person.
I will remind myself and everyone around
me that we don't have to be perfect,
we just have to keep trying to do
what is right and just.

PEACEMAKING IS NOT about getting everything right. Rather, it is the commitment to keep trying when you get it wrong. As a peacemaker, you commit to keep trying again and again. You will make mistakes. You will try and fail. You will say the wrong thing. You will get frustrated. You will want to give up. But as a peacemaker, you will find a way to keep going.

Failure and making mistakes are normal when creating a more just world. To keep trying means that you understand failure as learning. It means that you don't have to be perfect; you don't have to have all the answers or know what to do all the time. But you do have a responsibility to keep at it, to keep trying to find ways to make the world, and yourself, better.

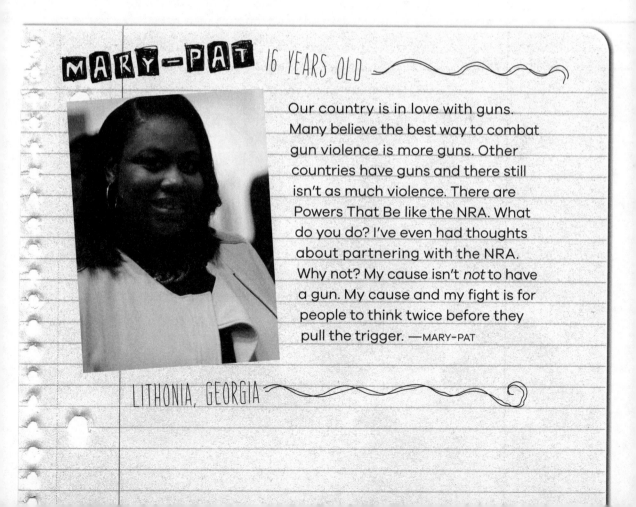

MARY-PAT 16 YEARS OLD

Our country is in love with guns. Many believe the best way to combat gun violence is more guns. Other countries have guns and there still isn't as much violence. There are Powers That Be like the NRA. What do you do? I've even had thoughts about partnering with the NRA. Why not? My cause isn't *not* to have a gun. My cause and my fight is for people to think twice before they pull the trigger. —MARY-PAT

LITHONIA, GEORGIA

Mary-Pat's activism started young. At her preschool graduation, the class speaker forgot the words of the speech she was supposed to give. Mary-Pat stood up next to her, held her hand, and began reciting the speech so her friend wouldn't feel embarrassed. That was the day she began wanting to help people.

When Mary-Pat was nine years old, a friend confided that she was being abused by her mom's boyfriend and made Mary-Pat swear she wouldn't tell. Wanting to keep her promise but also wanting to help her friend be safe, Mary-Pat found a shelter for kids facing abuse and asked them to intervene. At first they didn't take her seriously. Eventually they did and her friend was able to go live with her dad. Mary-Pat wondered, Why do adults not believe young people? Why don't they trust that young people can make a difference? Why do they only see young people as problems?

At eleven, Mary-Pat noticed a huge juvenile detention facility being built near her home to lock up young people who had gotten into trouble. At the same time, there were few places for young people to play, learn, and connect outside of school. A number of the large churches had recreation centers, but they didn't open their doors to area youth. Why was her community only investing in young people *after* they were in trouble, rather than providing amazing opportunities so they didn't get in trouble in the first place?

Mary-Pat organized a sit-in to get these community centers to open their doors to youth. Fifty young people joined her in sleeping outside for the weekend. She invited every politician, community leader, and television reporter she could find, but not one of them showed up. Dozens of young people spent an entire weekend sleeping on the streets to protest the lack of youth centers in their area and no one seemed to care. Those other young people lost hope and didn't know what to do.

To get people's attention, Mary-Pat called radio station after radio station, but no one would put her on the air. Station managers were surprised that young people wanted to make a difference. They assumed they just cared about music and fashion and their phones, not changing the world. Finally, Mary-Pat found a host who would put her on the

Mary-Pat tells her peacemaking story.

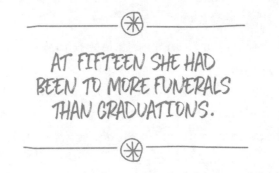

AT FIFTEEN SHE HAD BEEN TO MORE FUNERALS THAN GRADUATIONS.

radio to share her cause. But even with her pleas, the detention facility was built as planned.

One good thing came out of Mary-Pat's failed campaign. That radio host, a respected civil rights leader, invited her to meet with him. Mary-Pat challenged him on why his organization didn't have a youth component. Struck by her dedication, he asked, if she could change one thing in the world, what would it be?

Mary-Pat didn't need to think twice. For her the critical issue was gun violence and the devastating effect it had on young people and those around them. She knew, firsthand, the destruction that a single bullet could cause. At fifteen she had been to more funerals than graduations. But whenever she raised this issue with adults, she knew they would just throw up their hands. There was nothing to be done, they would say. This type of violence was inevitable.

Mary-Pat had seen "shock ads" on billboards around the city. These powerful images of the destructive effects of cigarettes and other drugs were meant to capture people's attention and move them to make different choices. Vivid pictures of young adults hooked up to machines in order to breathe because of smoking or teens who had died from drugs were hard to ignore. Why couldn't we do the same thing for gun violence? she wondered.

Mary-Pat's vision was the Think Twice campaign. She planned to

Mary-Pat (left) protesting gun violence in the streets of Atlanta.

use graphic images of the carnage of gun violence—children in caskets, grieving mothers—to shock people into making a different choice, to think twice before picking up a gun to hurt someone. If it worked for smoking, it could work for gun violence. Mary-Pat brought her idea to clergy, civil rights organizations, and community leaders around Atlanta and asked for their endorsement, funding, and connections to make this happen. Every single group she approached said no. They had other causes they cared about. Some thought showing these images would promote violence, not prevent it. Besides, she was just a kid. No one took her seriously. One civil rights leader even tried to take her idea and pass it off as her own.

After having her idea rejected again and again, Mary-Pat decided to do it on her own; but she still needed help and resources. To begin with, she had no idea how to actually design a billboard. She called every single advertising firm she could find. Most never even returned her calls. After dozens of tries, one finally called her back and offered to help bring her vision to life. Next she needed to raise the money to purchase billboard space. Mary-Pat reached out to everyone she knew—

multiple times. After months of trying, she finally raised enough money to put up a few billboards around Atlanta. Because gun violence affects everyone, she wanted the billboards to go in diverse parts of the city—rich areas, poor areas, middle-class areas. She wanted to spark a conversation.

Mary-Pat and former secretary of education Arne Duncan at a meeting about gun violence.

Even when she had money to buy billboard space, the company that controlled the city's billboards refused to put up Mary-Pat's ads. Executives at the company thought the images were too graphic and did not want it to seem as if they were promoting violence. The company was worried that gun supporters would be upset. Mary-Pat didn't understand. The company had put up racy billboards for strip clubs and rappers, but it rejected her images about gun violence prevention. They wanted to water down her message. In the end she had to compromise: she didn't get to use all of the pictures she wanted to, but she was able to keep the most important ones. For an entire summer her billboards were up in a few areas of the city.

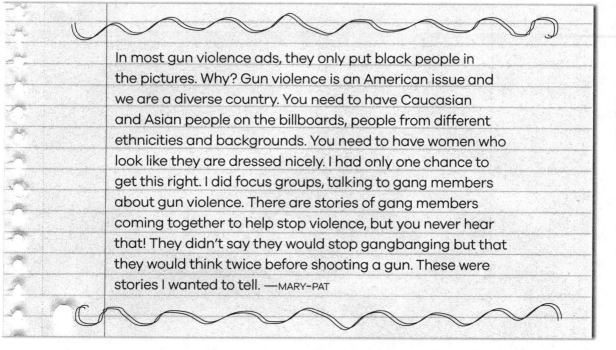

In most gun violence ads, they only put black people in the pictures. Why? Gun violence is an American issue and we are a diverse country. You need to have Caucasian and Asian people on the billboards, people from different ethnicities and backgrounds. You need to have women who look like they are dressed nicely. I had only one chance to get this right. I did focus groups, talking to gang members about gun violence. There are stories of gang members coming together to help stop violence, but you never hear that! They didn't say they would stop gangbanging but that they would think twice before shooting a gun. These were stories I wanted to tell. —MARY-PAT

And the billboards worked. Each year the Atlanta Police Department measures and reports on crime statistics from various city zones. When the next police department crime statistics were released, they showed a decrease in violence in the areas with Mary-Pat's billboards; in some blocks it was down significantly, even though violence usually increases during the summer. In areas without her billboards, gun violence stayed the same or went up.

But despite the billboards' success, Mary-Pat was unable to raise more money to keep them up. Raising money as a teenager is hard, and even the people who originally donated had moved on to other projects. After the summer, her billboards were taken down and replaced by the usual ones for pawnshops, car dealerships, and sports teams.

Mary-Pat remains committed to challenging people to think twice before they use guns to hurt someone else or themselves. She has taken her original billboard message—gun violence is something everyone should care about—and is now organizing groups of young people in different cities to carry this forward by speaking in schools and to community groups. She imagines a world where young people come together from rural, urban, and suburban areas and say "enough." She wants to get young people involved in taking back their communities. She has even thought about trying to partner with the country's largest gun rights advocacy organization, the National Rifle Association, to see if they could find common ground. With each "no," and every disappointment and dead end, Mary-Pat found a new route forward. With each failure, she learned how to make big change happen, better.

SHE IMAGINES A WORLD WHERE YOUNG PEOPLE COME TOGETHER FROM RURAL, URBAN, AND SUBURBAN AREAS AND SAY "ENOUGH."

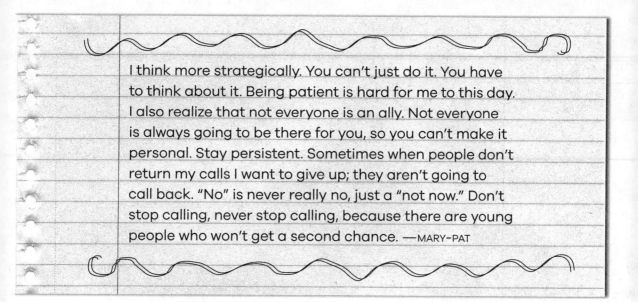

I think more strategically. You can't just do it. You have to think about it. Being patient is hard for me to this day. I also realize that not everyone is an ally. Not everyone is always going to be there for you, so you can't make it personal. Stay persistent. Sometimes when people don't return my calls I want to give up; they aren't going to call back. "No" is never really no, just a "not now." Don't stop calling, never stop calling, because there are young people who won't get a second chance. —MARY-PAT

A CLOSER LOOK

Mary-Pat would be the first to say that she has failed much more than she has succeeded, both with her project to end gun violence and in her daily interactions with others. It took her a long time to convince people that showing shocking images could reduce gun violence, and she had to compromise about which images would be used. Once she got the billboards up, even when data showed they were having a positive impact, she ran out of money. In a world where adults often don't take teens seriously, sometimes Mary-Pat gets so frustrated that she loses her temper and wants to give up.

The world, like the people in it, does not change easily. Unexpected curves, roadblocks, and frustrations shape journeys that look more like bowls of spaghetti than straight lines. And yet many of us expect straight lines; we want the path to be clear and easy. We tend to tell stories backward, from the point of success looking back, and everything seems to line up perfectly. But we live our stories forward, from where we are right now moving into uncertain futures, unsure what to do next. And yet we often don't allow ourselves to make mistakes.

When babies are just learning to stand and walk, they fall down all the time. No one gets upset, because they're supposed to fall down. That is how they learn. With each tumble their muscles become more coordinated and they understand more and more how their body works. Failing is part of the process of learning.

So it is with peacemaking. Being a peacemaker doesn't mean you need to be perfect. But you do have to keep trying to do what is right and just. Whether you lose your temper with a friend, have a person in power tell you no, or embarrass yourself in front of your class, failure is no excuse to stop trying. Rather, it is an invitation to learn, regroup, and try again.

★ **BE DRIVEN BUT ALSO BE PATIENT.** Being a peacemaker requires a commitment to act every day while understanding that change takes a long time. It is hard to do both of these—to be persistent and to be patient—and they can feel like opposites. But being patient doesn't mean you can't also push for justice. It does mean that you understand that people, including yourself, are often doing the best they can at that particular moment. And that it is enough. It took Mary-Pat many, many tries until she had the resources to put her billboards up, and even then she faced resistance and ultimately had to try a different path.

★ **BE PERSISTENT BUT ALSO BE FLEXIBLE.** Committing to being a peacemaker means you have to be dogged in your pursuit of a better world. At the same time, you need to be flexible in how you get there. If your first approach doesn't work out, talk to others who were involved to help understand why. What about your idea didn't work? Was it the idea itself, or was it how you implemented it? Or maybe both your idea and plan were solid, but they just needed more time to show success. Failure is not an excuse to give up. It's an opportunity to try another angle.

★ **BELIEVE IN YOURSELF BUT ALSO BE HUMBLE.** Your peacemaking work will be full of successes and failures. Just as you shouldn't lose hope with each setback, don't lose your sense of humility with each win. Humility is not about making yourself smaller or less great. It is about making space for other people's greatness. This means sharing decision making, sharing the mic, and sharing the credit. It is remembering that your successes, as well as your failures, are fleeting. Being a peacemaker requires an unwavering belief in the importance of your work while also understanding your own limitations. A win today doesn't guarantee one tomorrow.

Peacemaking is a marathon, not a sprint. And failure is often just the beginning of something great.

Advice from Mary-Pat

My advice is never give up. You will probably always have one or two people in your corner, but you will need to be your biggest cheerleader. Don't let anyone tell you that you can't. Always dream big.

FROM COMMITMENT → TO ACTION

REFLECT:

Think back on the story and ideas about this commitment.

1. What did you notice about Mary-Pat's story? Do you feel like she failed?

2. What were the obstacles that Mary-Pat faced? How did she overcome them? How did she keep from giving up?

3. Who were some of the people who helped Mary-Pat along the way? Who stood in her way and made her journey more difficult?

TAKE STOCK:

Think about yourself, honestly, and what you know to be true right now.

1. When was a time that you failed and what did you learn from that moment? How did it feel? How did others react?

2. When was a time that you gave up because a project felt too hard or too big? What did you learn from that moment?

3. Who are people you turn to when you are feeling unsuccessful? Who turns to you?

TAKE ACTION:

Think about how you will apply the commitment to keep trying in your everyday life. Below are three ideas to get you started.

1. Right now I will no longer try to be perfect but instead commit to getting better each and every day.

2. Tomorrow I will apologize to one person I have hurt while moving too fast or trying to get something right.

3. Every day I will write down one mistake I made, think of one thing I will do differently tomorrow, then rip it up.

WHAT ELSE MIGHT YOU TRY?

PUTTING IT TOGETHER

> *Peacemaking is mobilizing others to be leaders for the greater good. If you want something to change you have to do it, you have to start it. Show people how to do it with your actions and then they will follow.* —DANIELLE

WHILE PEACEMAKING IS an everyday activity—how you welcome new people at school, how you deal with conflict among your friends, or how you react to frustrations and disappointments—it is also applying these commitments to tackle bigger problems you see in the world. In addition to putting peace first in your daily life, being a peacemaker means working with others to solve bigger challenges. These are called *PEACEMAKING PROJECTS*.

A peacemaking project seeks to solve an injustice in the world using compassion and courage. What makes a successful peacemaking project isn't the size or scale, but how you apply the commitments of peacemaking to make the world a better place. Taking a stand for what you believe in. Working to understand different people's perspectives. Including others, particularly people who disagree with you. A peacemaking project is different from other service projects or volunteer work because it is equal parts what you do and who you are while doing it. And while being a peacemaker is an ongoing journey, peacemaking projects have a start and a finish, offering a chance to reflect on what you've done and what you might want to do next.

You've explored the different commitments and skills it takes to be a peacemaker. Now it's time to put your peacemaking skills into action.

TIPS FOR BUILDING A TEAM

PEACEMAKING PROJECTS ARE STRONGER WITH OTHER PEOPLE. HERE ARE SOME THINGS TO KEEP IN MIND WHEN BUILDING A TEAM:

— START WITH WHO YOU KNOW. RECRUIT A FEW TRUSTED FRIENDS WHO YOU ENJOY SPENDING TIME WITH AND WHO SHARE YOUR PASSIONS.

— REACH OUT TO SOMEONE YOU DON'T KNOW AS WELL, BUT WHO YOU THINK MIGHT WORK WITH YOU ON A PROJECT.

— CONSIDER INCLUDING PEOPLE YOU WOULDN'T USUALLY WORK WITH. MAYBE SOMEONE FROM A DIFFERENT FRIEND GROUP. OR SOMEONE YOU DON'T ALWAYS GET ALONG WITH. YOU NEVER KNOW WHO MIGHT BRING THE TALENT AND CONNECTIONS YOU NEED FOR SUCCESS.

SIX STEPS FOR IMAGINING AND IMPLEMENTING A PEACEMAKING PROJECT:

CHOOSE. What injustice or problem do you really care about, and why is it important?

UNDERSTAND. What is the root cause of the problem and how do others feel about it?

IMAGINE. How might you solve the problem using courage and compassion?

PLAN. How can you break the solution into concrete steps with a clear timeline and invite others to join you?

ACT. What happens when you hit bumps in the road?

REFLECT. How are you different because of your peacemaking work? How has your peacemaking work affected others?

IT'S TIME TO GET STARTED!

STEP 1:
CHOOSE AN INJUSTICE

> *First, find your issue that is most personal to you. If it isn't personal, then it isn't real or authentic. It doesn't help anyone if you join something just for the sake of joining. Find what is most personal. Read up on it. Do your research. Start interacting with people who are adamant about solving whatever is personal to them. I'm a firm believer not to jump to other people's causes that you can't speak to.* —BABATUNDE

What is an issue or problem that you care about? It needs to be an *injustice*: an issue that truly hurts or holds back a group of people. And it needs to be an issue where you can make a difference. You may already know exactly what you want to tackle. You may have no idea. You may sit somewhere in between and have a sense that something bothers you, but you don't know how to describe it.

EXPLORE WHAT YOU CARE ABOUT. Perhaps, as with Babatunde and the police, there is an issue that has happened to you directly, something that has made you feel sad, angry, or hurt. Perhaps, as with Jeremiah and his school's cyberbullying, there is an issue that doesn't affect you directly but hurts others around you. Or maybe you have read or heard about a problem, something that makes you so angry that you feel a need to act, even if you don't have any direct experience with it. What matters is that this issue is important to you and you want to make a difference.

Think about your school, neighborhood, and the world around you. What are the best things about it? What makes it great? Who are the people and organizations that do good things, who make life better for other people? Make a list of ten good things you see happening that you want more of.

Now think about the problems in your school, neighborhood, and the world around you. What feels broken? Where do you see people hurt, sad, or treated unfairly? Where are people excluded or made to feel inferior? Where do these problems come from? Who are the people and groups who cause them? Make a list of ten bad or unfair things you want to stop or change.

Look at both of these lists. Is there a pattern to them, something that appears a few times in different ways? Is there a connection between something you want to see more of and something you want to stop? Read through the list again and cross out items that feel less important and circle ones that feel more important. Read through the list one more time and choose the issue that most resonates with you.

IS THE ISSUE YOU HAVE CHOSEN AN INJUSTICE OR MERELY AN INCONVENIENCE? An injustice is a problem that causes long-term harm to a group of people. Often this group is specifically targeted simply because of who they are, where they are from, or what they look like. The harm is caused by other people or by unfair laws or rules that prevent the targeted group from feeling safe and happy. Both Mary-Pat and Katebah realized that gun violence was devastating entire neighborhoods, breaking down community bonds, and making people feel unsafe. Matthew realized not just that bullying was making his brother's life miserable, but that many other students were experiencing the exact same thing.

An inconvenience, on the other hand, is a fleeting problem that minimally affects others. It is often short-term or limited. If your school has a dress code you don't like, that's an inconvenience. If your school has a dress code that unfairly singles out girls, that's an injustice because it is a rule that targets one group of people and reinforces stereotypes. A problem doesn't need to be big to be an injustice; it needs only to be rooted in unfairness and affect other people. Look at your issue again. If your problem seems more like an inconvenience, ask yourself: What bigger issue might this problem be connected to?

IN CHOOSING THE PROBLEM YOU WANT TO ADDRESS, YOU SHOULD BE ABLE TO ANSWER THESE THREE QUESTIONS:

☐ DOES THIS ISSUE CAUSE LONG-TERM HARM TO A GROUP OF PEOPLE?

☐ IS THIS GROUP TARGETED BECAUSE OF WHO THEY ARE, WHERE THEY ARE FROM, OR WHAT THEY LOOK LIKE?

☐ IS THE HARM CAUSED BY OTHER PEOPLE, LAWS, OR RULES?

CAN YOU MAKE A DIFFERENCE WORKING ON THIS INJUSTICE?

Making a difference doesn't mean that you will be able to end the entire injustice; it means you can envision the possibility of making a change, that you have a sense of how you want to improve the problem. Ask yourself: Can I, with help from others, make this problem better? If the answer is no, if the problem feels too big, can you find a smaller piece of the problem to start with? Mary-Pat didn't begin with tackling gun violence across the country but focused on neighborhoods in Atlanta. Danielle worked to break down barriers between people with and without disabilities, even though there were many other divisions on her college campus that also needed attention.

TAKE ANOTHER LOOK AT THE PROBLEM YOU HAVE CHOSEN AND CONFIRM: Does this matter to you? Is it an injustice—does it cause long-term harm to others? Can you imagine making a difference? If you can answer yes to all three questions, you are ready to go deeper into understanding the root of your problem. Remember, your idea doesn't have to be perfect. It is just a starting point, and your understanding of the issue will deepen over time. Peacemakers often start on one injustice and end up tackling others as they learn and gain experience.

STEP 2:

UNDERSTAND THE ROOT CAUSE

> *It is really important to continue to ask the question why. Why does it happen? The more you can trace back, asking why, why, and why again, the closer you can get to understanding. You need to ask people who see the world differently from you, who grew up in a world different from yours.* —MATTHEW

Injustices are like trees. There are parts that we see and there are parts underneath that aren't always visible. You want to understand the roots of your problem. The best way to do this is by listening to the perspectives of both those affected by the problem and those involved in creating it. It is easy to divide the world into good people who help and bad people who harm. But the truth is, to create any lasting solution you need the viewpoints of everyone involved—those who want to help and those who might want to stop you. This will allow you to understand the complexity of the problem, its various causes, and how it affects other people. An effort, grounded in compassion, to address the root cause of an injustice is what distinguishes a peacemaking project from other good efforts.

For Wei this meant understanding that the students who were terrorizing him and his friends were also victims of a deep-seated culture of violence at his school. For Danielle, it meant realizing that students were teasing others with disabilities not because they were bad people but because they had not spent real time getting to know someone with a disability. And for Jeremiah, it meant discovering that while social media made it easy to spread nasty comments, it could also be a force for good. In each one of these examples the problem—school violence, disability discrimination, cyberbullying—was solved by understanding a critical root cause—school culture, lack of exposure, student negativity—not just addressing symptoms. And each cause was uncovered through compassion—understanding the points of views of others.

RESEARCH TO LEARN MORE ABOUT YOUR INJUSTICE. Look at what others are already doing and what they have learned. Explore their discoveries. What do people generally agree on, and where are points of disagreement? Ask others what they think about the problem, including people who might disagree with you. Who is most affected by the injustice in your community? What other people or groups are also concerned about it? Who is most responsible for creating this problem? Who benefits from it? Who agrees with you and wants to help? Who disagrees with you and might stand in your way?

What can you learn from both groups? Try to interview at least five people.

ORGANIZE ALL YOU HAVE LEARNED BY MAKING A PROBLEM TREE.

Draw a tree. In the center, write the injustice you have chosen to tackle. In the branches, write all of the **CONSEQUENCES OF THE PROBLEM**: What harm does it cause? Who does it hurt and how? Where do you see the harm being caused? Consider the research you have done and what you heard from other people. Give yourself ninety seconds to write down as many ideas as you can think of as quickly as you can, then read what you wrote. Do this three times, each time going broader and deeper to explore the full range of consequences caused by the problem.

Then in the roots consider the following: Why does this problem exist? What causes it? Who causes it? Look in the branches at all of the consequences you uncovered—what makes all of them possible? Consider the research you have done and what you heard from other people. Give yourself ninety seconds to write down as many **ROOT CAUSES OF THE PROBLEM** as you can think of as quickly as you can, then read what you wrote. Do this three times, each time going deeper and deeper into the roots of the injustice. Don't worry about getting it perfect; the goal is to get out as many ideas as you can, based on what you know and what you have learned.

* NEW KIDS HAVE A HARD TIME FITTING IN.

* STUDENTS CAN'T BE THEMSELVES, AND FEEL ASHAMED.

* KIDS WHO BULLY OTHERS GET IN TROUBLE AND MISS SCHOOL. PEOPLE DON'T LIKE THEM.

* SOME KIDS DROP OUT OR HURT THEMSELVES BECAUSE THEY ARE SAD.

* EVEN KIDS WHO AREN'T INVOLVED ARE TOO SCARED TO SPEAK UP BECAUSE THEY MIGHT BE NEXT.

* EVERYONE GETS THE MESSAGE THAT IF YOU AREN'T A "TYPICAL" KID YOU ARE WORTHLESS.

* KIDS WHO ARE BULLIED MISS SCHOOL AND THEIR GRADES SUFFER.

* BULLIED KIDS HAVE FEWER FRIENDS.

EXAMPLE: BULLIES AT MY SCHOOL HURT PEOPLE WHO SEEM DIFFERENT.

* SOCIETY'S DEFINITION OF "NORMAL" IS LIMITED TO ONLY SPECIFIC TYPES OF PEOPLE.

* TEACHERS LOOK THE OTHER WAY, OR WORSE, THEY LAUGH TOO.

* PEOPLE EXCUSE THE BEHAVIOR— THAT'S JUST HOW KIDS ARE.

* THERE'S TOO MUCH PRESSURE AT SCHOOL TO FIT IN.

* KIDS WHO BULLY FEEL BAD ABOUT THEMSELVES AND TAKE IT OUT ON OTHERS.

* STUDENTS WHO SEE IT HAPPENING LAUGH ALONG OR DO NOTHING.

* SOCIAL MEDIA ALLOWS FOR ANONYMOUS WAYS TO BE MEAN.

After you have finished, take a moment to look at all of the root causes you have identified. Do you see an overall pattern? Which one feels most important? Which one do you want to tackle first? Circle the two or three that feel most important. See if you can write this idea into a summary sentence. For Katebah, her root cause might read, "A lack of community leads to violence." For Danielle: "A lack of meaningful connection between people with and without disabilities leads to mistrust and mistreatment." For Mary-Pat: "Gun violence has become so commonplace that people are no longer shocked by shootings." How would you describe the root cause of your problem?

TAKE ONE FINAL LOOK AT THE ROOT CAUSE YOU HAVE CHOSEN. Do you see a clear connection between this insight and the injustice you want to solve? Do you feel passionate about changing it? Through understanding the roots of the problem you care about, you can begin to find the kernel of a solution.

TIPS FOR INTERVIEWS

INTERVIEWING OTHER PEOPLE CAN BE HARD; INTERVIEWING PEOPLE WHO SEE THE WORLD DIFFERENTLY FROM YOU CAN BE EVEN HARDER. HERE ARE A FEW HINTS:

— BE GRACIOUS: THANK THE PERSON OR GROUP YOU ARE INTERVIEWING BEFORE AND AFTER THE INTERVIEW.

— ASK OPEN-ENDED QUESTIONS THAT CANNOT BE ANSWERED WITH A "YES" OR A "NO."

— BE PREPARED TO HEAR THINGS THAT MAKE YOU FEEL UNCOMFORTABLE. LISTEN FROM THE HEART AS WELL AS THE HEAD; AIM TO UNDERSTAND WHY SOMEONE FEELS THE WAY THEY FEEL.

STEP 3:
IMAGINE A SOLUTION

> *Make sure your solution fits the uniqueness of your issue. Look at what other people are doing, but don't feel you need to copy it. Don't be afraid to think differently, to be that dreamer, to be a little crazy. It takes a certain amount of madness to change the world.* —JEREMIAH

The solution for any injustice can be found within the root of the problem itself. Once you know what causes it, you can figure out how to change it. Once Katebah understood that it was a lack of community that was driving the violence, she knew she had to focus on connecting people to one another. Babatunde realized the police and young people of color not only didn't trust each other but they didn't know each other. Therefore he designed workshops to create empathy. For Mary-Pat it was the fact that gun violence had become commonplace, which meant she needed to shock people out of their complacency. Each peacemaker's solution was grounded in how they understood the root of the injustice. So it is for all peacemaking projects.

IMAGINE WHAT THE WORLD WILL LOOK LIKE WHEN YOU'RE SUCCESSFUL BY CREATING A SOLUTION TREE. Draw a second tree. This time, rather than writing the problem in its trunk, write its opposite. What is a powerful alternative to the injustice you identified? What do you want the world to look like? For Wei, it might be a school in which everyone feels safe and cared for. For Babatunde, it might be a police culture built on real partnerships with young people of color.

In the tree's branches, write all of the effects of your alternative: If this happens, whom will it affect and how? How will your original injustice be different? How will the world be better? Give yourself ninety seconds to write down as many ideas as you can think of as quickly as you can, then read what you wrote. Do this three times, each time going broader and broader to explore the full range of outcomes when the problem is fixed.

On the tree's roots, write possible solutions: What would cause this positive change? How might you make it happen? Who would need to be involved to help? What activities would be most helpful? Give yourself ninety seconds to write down as many ideas as you can think of as quickly as you can, then read what you wrote. Do this three times, each time going deeper and deeper to explore the roots of the positive outcome you want to see happen. These are your possible solutions.

EFFECTS: HOW WILL THE SOLUTION MAKE THE WORLD BETTER?

POSITIVE ALTERNATIVE: WHAT DO YOU WANT THE WORLD TO LOOK LIKE?

POSSIBLE SOLUTIONS: WHAT WILL CAUSE THIS POSITIVE CHANGE?

* NO MATTER WHAT YOU LOOK LIKE, YOU FEEL THAT YOU BELONG.

* KIDS WILL WANT TO COME TO SCHOOL.

* BULLYING WON'T BE ACCEPTED, AND BULLIES WON'T GET IN TROUBLE.

* GRADES WILL BE BETTER BECAUSE TEACHERS CAN TEACH.

* THERE WILL BE LESS DEPRESSION AND SUICIDE.

KIDS WHO ARE DIFFERENT ARE ACCEPTED AND RESPECTED.

* SCHOOL-WIDE TRAINING TEACHES ABOUT APPRECIATING DIFFERENCES.

* POSITIVE MESSAGES ABOUT DIFFERENCES FROM MOVIES, TV, SOCIAL MEDIA.

* TEACHERS INTERVENE IN SUPPORTIVE WAYS.

* STUDENTS WHO SEE BULLYING HAPPENING STEP IN TO STOP IT.

* BULLIES FEEL SUPPORTED AND LOVED, SO THEY STOP HURTING OTHERS.

CONSIDER ALL OF THE SOLUTIONS YOU HAVE IMAGINED. Do you see an overall pattern? Does one feel more important than the others? Which idea are you most excited about? Cross out those that feel repetitive or undoable. Circle the ones that feel most effective and possible. See if you can write this idea into one summary sentence. For Matthew it might look like this: "Interactive workshops where people learn about one another in safe and fun ways lead to people feeling connected and cared for." For Jeremiah: "Sincere compliments restore connection and community." In doing this, you are uncovering the solution you will create to solve your identified problem.

WHAT WILL HELP YOU SUCCEED, AND WHAT STANDS IN YOUR WAY?

Place your two trees side by side. Imagine moving from the problem tree to the solution tree. Between the trees, make a list of who or what will get in your way and who or what will help you succeed. In other words, what forces are committed to keeping the problem the way it is and what forces want to make it better? Are there challenges that you will have to overcome to be successful? Are there people who are adding to the problem that you might work with to create a solution? What people or groups might agree with your idea and offer help? Try to list as many different forces as possible, both those that help move you toward your solution and those that stand in the way. You may end up working on strengthening the helpers or weakening the blockers. Or both.

PROBLEM: BULLIES HURT PEOPLE WHO SEEM DIFFERENT

WHO OR WHAT WILL HELP YOU SUCCEED?

* KIDS AND TEACHERS WHO FEEL THE SAME WAY AND WANT TO HELP.

* KIDS AND TEACHERS WHO INTERVENE IN POSITIVE WAYS.

* YOUNG PEOPLE, BECAUSE THEY LISTEN TO OTHER YOUNG PEOPLE MORE THAN THEY DO ADULTS.

* A WORKSHOP ABOUT TOLERANCE AND INCLUSION LED BY YOUNG PEOPLE.

WHO OR WHAT WILL GET IN YOUR WAY?

* SOME KIDS AND TEACHERS DON'T CARE.
* TYPICAL ADULT-LED PRESENTATIONS ARE BORING.
* ATTEMPTS TO PUNISH BULLIES DON'T WORK.
* ADULTS DON'T TAKE YOUTHS SERIOUSLY.

SOLUTION: KIDS WHO ARE DIFFERENT ARE ACCEPTED AND RESPECTED

As you look at this list of forces, pick two or three that you want to focus on. Which feel most important to your success? You can bring other forces in later, but decide which ones you want to begin with. For Katebah, building community through shared sacrifice felt most powerful. For Matthew, having young people—rather than adults—teach other young people about kindness was a driving force. Babatunde knew he would have to overcome police officers' resistance to being taught by a teenager. Understanding the forces that will hold your solution back and those that will propel it forward is critical as you turn your idea into a plan.

REVIEW THE SOLUTION YOU HAVE SELECTED. Does it feel brave and compassionate? Will it make a difference? Do the forces you have identified feel like the most important ones to consider as you make your plans? Together, the solution and the forces will remind you of how you want to reshape the world.

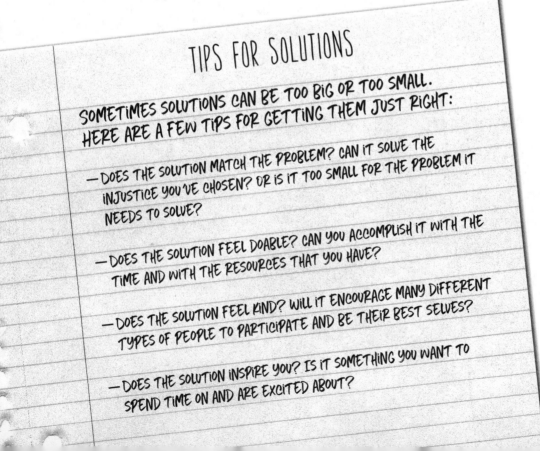

TIPS FOR SOLUTIONS

SOMETIMES SOLUTIONS CAN BE TOO BIG OR TOO SMALL.
HERE ARE A FEW TIPS FOR GETTING THEM JUST RIGHT:

—DOES THE SOLUTION MATCH THE PROBLEM? CAN IT SOLVE THE INJUSTICE YOU'VE CHOSEN? OR IS IT TOO SMALL FOR THE PROBLEM IT NEEDS TO SOLVE?

—DOES THE SOLUTION FEEL DOABLE? CAN YOU ACCOMPLISH IT WITH THE TIME AND WITH THE RESOURCES THAT YOU HAVE?

—DOES THE SOLUTION FEEL KIND? WILL IT ENCOURAGE MANY DIFFERENT TYPES OF PEOPLE TO PARTICIPATE AND BE THEIR BEST SELVES?

—DOES THE SOLUTION INSPIRE YOU? IS IT SOMETHING YOU WANT TO SPEND TIME ON AND ARE EXCITED ABOUT?

STEP 4:
MAKE A PLAN

> *I love advocacy. It is so easy to send out just one email. The person you think will be most helpful may not be, but you can't exclude anyone. Someone will always help with something. I tell my classmates, 'Email people, tell them what you are doing, don't be ashamed.' That's how a movement happens. People tell their people.* —KATEBAH

Even the most amazing solutions are meaningless without a plan to turn them into reality. There is nothing mysterious about creating a plan. You do it all the time, whether organizing homework assignments, bringing together your friends for an activity, or simply deciding which movie to watch with your family. Planning involves making decisions about your end goal—where to start and what to do next—as well as whom to involve and what resources you will need.

A good plan is your best guess about how to achieve your solution. As you begin, focus on your end goal and work backward. Break your project down into doable steps and understand what resources—money, supplies, time—you will need. And don't forget to reach out to and involve people who can help you. The best plans create opportunities for others to add their visions and skills too.

SET YOUR FiRST GOAL. Keeping your solution in mind, start by defining a goal that feels doable and works to solve your injustice. Decide what success looks like and where you want to get first. Consider the forces you identified that will help or hinder your work. How can you account for them as you get started? Danielle didn't start with the goal of building the largest student club at her college with hundreds of participants. She was aiming to find twenty-four students to play basketball together so they could connect. Babatunde didn't start off wanting to train hundreds of police officers. He began with setting up conversations with a small group of officers so that they could learn from each other. Set the first goal for solving your injustice by being S.M.A.R.T.:

S. M. A. R. T.

SPECIFIC. What exactly do you want to achieve as your first major step? Make sure it is concrete. When people hear your goal, they should know what you are trying to accomplish.

MEASURABLE. How will you know if you're successful? Describe your goal in terms of numbers or time so you can track your progress.

ATTAINABLE. Can you achieve your goal with the time and the resources you have? This doesn't mean you can't think big. It means that you should set an initial goal that feels doable.

RELEVANT. Does your goal connect with your passion and energy? You and the people helping you should be excited to get started.

TIME-BOUND. By when will you achieve your goal? Set clear start, middle, and end times.

As with all of your planning, it isn't about getting everything perfect as much as it is getting started. Matthew's first goal was to create a two-hour empathy workshop for his brother's class. Jeremiah recruited ten other students to help him tweet compliments. What is your first major goal for your peacemaking project? What opportunity or change do you want to achieve first?

CREATE A PLAN TO ACHIEVE THIS FIRST GOAL. Keeping track of everything you need to do in order to reach a goal can quickly start to feel overwhelming. Rather than thinking of your plan as a long list of steps, think about your plan as a person, with each part representing a different piece of your planning work. This way you can see how everything fits together.

Start by drawing an outline of a person.

ABOVE THE PERSON: Write the first goal you have identified for solving your injustice.

ON THE HEAD: List two or three specific things you need to learn more about and how you will get this information. Maybe you want to understand even more about the history of the problem or identify community resources that can help. Perhaps you are curious about how others have created similar projects in other places. Or maybe you have no idea how to write a business letter or do a presentation for adults. Identify the most important things you need to learn to achieve your goal.

ON ONE HAND: Since you will need more than just yourself and your ideas to be successful, name two or three people or groups you will reach out and ask to join you. Who can help you achieve your first goal? How can you bring them along? Maybe you need permission from your principal to hold an assembly or the help of three friends to distribute posters. Who do you need on your team and how can you get them on board?

ON THE OTHER HAND: List at least three key resources you need to achieve the goal. This could be supplies like paint or basketballs. It could be money or access to equipment like cameras or shovels. What specific items do you need and how can you get them?

ON ONE FOOT: Write the key steps or milestones for reaching your first goal. To reach your goal, what do you need to do first? And next after that? Perhaps you want to begin by inviting others to a kick-off meeting. Other tasks could include writing a lesson plan, contacting a refugee center to explore a partnership, or writing fundraising letters for area businesses. While there will be lots of small tasks, try to identify the most important steps for achieving your goal.

ON THE OTHER FOOT: Write two to three measures for knowing you've been successful. They should be easy to communicate and confirm. Perhaps the number of people who sign your petition or attend your event. Or the rate of reduction for school suspensions or trash in the park. How will you tell when you've accomplished your goal?

OVER THE HEART: Add two or three steps you will take to make sure you continue to listen and understand other people's points of view throughout your project. How might you get feedback from others on a regular basis? How can you deepen your understanding of how the problem affects other people? What specific steps can you take to create more understanding for both yourself and others?

GOAL: THE OPPORTUNITY OR CHANGE YOU WANT TO ACHIEVE FIRST

I WILL LEARN MORE ABOUT . . .

I WILL UNDERSTAND OTHERS BY . . .

OTHER PEOPLE I NEED TO JOIN ME ARE . . .

SUPPLIES AND RESOURCES I NEED ARE . . .

KEY STEPS ARE . . .

I'LL KNOW I'M SUCCESSFUL BECAUSE . . .

GOAL: CREATE A YOUTH-LED WORKSHOP ABOUT ACCEPTANCE THAT WILL BE GIVEN TO INDIVIDUAL CLASSES AT SCHOOL

I WILL LEARN MORE ABOUT:

* WHY PEOPLE BULLY.
* LAWS ABOUT BULLYING.
* FUN ACTIVITIES THAT BUILD TOLERANCE.

I WILL UNDERSTAND OTHERS BY:

* TALKING WITH SOMEONE WHO HAS BEEN BULLIED.
* TALKING WITH A BULLY.
* TALKING WITH A TEACHER.

OTHER PEOPLE I NEED TO JOIN ME ARE:

* FOUR PEOPLE TO RUN SMALL GROUPS.
* A TEACHER TO REVIEW OUR WORKSHOP OUTLINE.

SUPPLIES AND RESOURCES I NEED ARE:

* PERMISSION TO TEACH WORK-SHOPS FOR SIXTH GRADERS.
* A LIST OF ICEBREAKERS.
* ROLE-PLAYING EXAMPLES OF BULLYING.
* STATISTICS TO SHARE.
* BASIC ART SUPPLIES (CRAYONS, PAPER, GLUE).

KEY STEPS ARE:

* RECRUITING FOUR FRIENDS TO HELP ME.
* INTERVIEWING KIDS WHO HAVE BEEN BULLIED AND KIDS WHO HAVE BULLIED.
* WRITING AN OVERVIEW OF MY GOALS AND AGENDA AND GETTING FEEDBACK ABOUT MY OVERVIEW FROM A TEACHER.
* SETTING A WORKSHOP DATE.
* TEACHING THE LESSON!
* GATHERING FEEDBACK AFTER THE WORKSHOP.
* FIGURING OUT IF WE WANT TO DO MORE.

I'LL KNOW I'M SUCCESSFUL BECAUSE:

* FIFTY STUDENTS TRAIN TO ACCEPT PEOPLE WHO ARE DIFFERENT.
* QUESTIONNAIRES BEFORE AND AFTER THE WORKSHOP SHOW INCREASED STUDENT ACCEPTANCE.
* TEACHERS AND STUDENTS RECOMMEND THE WORKSHOP TO OTHERS.
* A MONTH LATER STUDENTS REMEMBER WHAT THEY LEARNED.

CHECK YOUR PLAN. Do the steps, resources, and ideas you've identified make sense together? Does it feel doable? Does it feel like anything is missing? Once you get started implementing your project, you will be able to return to your plan to plot next steps and revise actions as you learn more.

TIPS FOR EVENTS

EVENTS CAN BE AN IMPORTANT PART OF PEACEMAKING PROJECTS. THEY CAN RAISE AWARENESS, BRING PEOPLE TOGETHER, AND INSPIRE OTHERS TO JOIN YOUR CAUSE. HERE ARE SOME POINTS TO THINK ABOUT:

— IDENTIFY A DATE, TIME, AND PLACE THAT WILL ALLOW THE MOST PEOPLE TO ATTEND.

— WHO DO YOU WANT TO COME? IS THERE SOMEONE YOU MIGHT NOT BE THINKING OF?

— WHAT RESOURCES AND MATERIALS DO YOU NEED? HOW CAN YOU GET THOSE ITEMS?

— FIND OUT IF THERE IS ANOTHER EVENT HAPPENING THAT YOU CAN JOIN FORCES WITH.

STEP 5:
ACT

> *During my struggle, adults played a huge role for me. Some were trying to destroy my dreams and stop me. Others believed in me, trusted me that I could lead, helped me to lead it. Both types were key to my success because they pushed me to be a leader.* —WEI

After all of your thinking and organizing, it is time to put your ideas into action. Put down the book and go out in the world and work toward your goal. Do remember: Turning a plan into reality can be both exciting and hard. You might notice that ideas you thought would be easy turn out to be challenging to implement. On the other hand, steps you thought might take a long time might move quickly. Throughout the project, keep returning to your solution, your first big goal, and your planning design for guidance. As you work on your peacemaking project, keep these things in mind:

EXPECT ROADBLOCKS. There will be people who do not want you to succeed: people who are invested in keeping the injustice in place, people who are jealous of what you are accomplishing, people who don't seem to care as much as you do. There will be people who promise to help but let you down. You will follow paths that become dead ends, and you'll need to discover a different way through. It took Wei two years to figure out how to organize his fellow students. Jeremiah received threats from other students for the work he was doing. It took Katebah many tries to convince community activists that her model was worth a try. Few people took Mary-Pat seriously, and billboard company after billboard company turned her down.

No peacemaking journey is a smooth one. Ideally, all peacemaking projects would be successful. They aren't. Each step in your peacemaking project is not about getting it right but getting smarter. Constantly try out new approaches, learn from your experiences, and adapt. Listen and pay attention. Stay committed, but keep an open mind when confronted with a change in direction. And don't work alone. Successes are always sweeter, and setbacks are always better dealt with, when you're joined by others who share your vision and commitment.

ADULTS CAN BE COMPLICATED. The adults around you are learning too and may be unsure of what their role should be in your peacemaking project. They may try too hard to be supportive, taking over rather than letting you lead. Others may try too little, not showing much interest. Still others may discount and dismiss the role young people can play in solving problems and thwart your efforts to create positive change. Most of the adults at Wei's school dismissed him as a troublemaker. Matthew's parents wanted to help but didn't know how. Mary-Pat eventually found a few adults who were willing to help her, but most thought what she wanted to do was impossible.

On the other hand, adult help can be invaluable. They can provide access to resources, terrific advice, comfort when you are frustrated, and cheer when you succeed. Babatunde had strong mentors in his after-school program. Wei had community leaders who lent their credibility, support, and organizing experience. Katebah had teachers who helped plan, gather resources, and join in the fast. The key is to be clear with adult supporters about the type of help you need and the type you don't. Engage and appreciate mentors at critical stages and don't lose hope if it takes a few tries to get it right. You are asking adults to engage with young people in a way that may be very different from what they are used to. They need time to learn, make mistakes, and try again too.

TAKE RISKS BUT STAY SAFE. All peacemaking work involves risks. Babatunde took a risk reaching out to train police officers. Matthew took a risk standing up in front of his brother's middle school classroom to run a workshop. Danielle took a risk bringing two groups of people together that had a rocky history. By definition, peacemaking work is about crossing boundaries, standing up for others, and opening your heart—all risky ventures.

Most of the risks are limited—looking silly in front of your friends, not having kindness reciprocated. But some are significant—angering people in power, pushing yourself and others beyond your breaking point, putting yourself and others in physically unsafe environments. There is a line between taking important risks and being reckless. You need to understand and explore this line. With each step in your work, ask yourself: Am I putting myself or others at risk? If the answer is yes, follow up with these questions: Is this a short-term, temporary risk that will help me grow as a peacemaker, or is this risk too dangerous? What is one thing I can do or change to make this risk smaller?

People are often poor judges of personal risk. They tend to either overestimate it (this is way too dangerous; we shouldn't even try) and therefore don't push themselves to do more, or they underestimate it (What's the worst that can happen? Let's do it!) and put themselves in real danger. Ask a mentor or friend, someone you trust and with whom you can think through options and ideas, to be your risk buddy. You don't need to make your peacemaking project risk-free; but you do need to ensure your safety and the safety of those working with you.

TIPS FOR SHARING YOUR STORY

AS YOU WORK ON YOUR PROJECT, REMEMBER TO CAPTURE KEY MOMENTS TO SHARE WITH OTHERS. BY SHARING YOUR STORY YOU WILL INSPIRE OTHERS TO TAKE A STAND. HERE ARE A FEW IDEAS FOR RECORDING YOUR EXPERIENCES:

—FIND THE MEDIUM YOU ARE MOST COMFORTABLE WITH. IT MIGHT BE WRITING, PHOTOS, VIDEO, MUSIC, ANYTHING! BE CREATIVE.

—PLAN AND PRACTICE BEFORE SHARING. YOU DON'T HAVE TO BE PERFECT, BUT YOU SHOULD BE THOUGHTFUL. MAKE SURE THE MATERIAL FEELS RIGHT FOR THE AUDIENCE.

—TRY TO BE CONCISE. FOCUS ON KEY IDEAS SUCH AS WHY THIS ISSUE IS IMPORTANT TO YOU AND YOUR COMMUNITY, AND WHAT CHALLENGES YOU ENCOUNTERED.

—SHARE YOUR STORY IN A VARIETY OF VENUES, WHETHER THROUGH SOCIAL MEDIA, AT A SCHOOL BOARD MEETING, OR AMONG YOUR FRIENDS.

STEP 6:
REFLECT ON WHAT HAPPENED

When you complete your first goal (or decide that a new goal is needed based on what you have learned), this is the perfect moment to pause. Celebrate what has happened, share what you have learned, and imagine what could happen next. While reflecting may not feel like "real" work, it is as essential as any other part of your peacemaking project. Through reflection, we deepen our own learning and express gratitude to those who have joined us on the journey.

WHAT HAPPENED? Gather your partners and, together, tell the story of what has happened so far. What have you achieved? What have you learned? How is your community different? How are you different? What is a moment that you are really proud of? What would you do differently? What have you learned about the injustice? Which of your original assumptions still feel right and true? What feels different or new?

APPRECIATE THOSE WHO HAVE HELPED. Express gratitude for the people who helped you with your project. This might take the form of a thank-you note, a public appreciation, or a simple acknowledgment to your team. This is especially important for those less involved in your peacemaking project, who might not know the impact they have had. And don't forget to appreciate yourself and reflect on all you have accomplished!

IMAGINE WHAT'S NEXT. Revisit your original plans and thinking. What still feels right about it? What should be different? As you reexamine the root cause and the solution, what have you learned? Look back at the forces that drive toward a solution and the forces that get in the way. As you complete your first big goal, imagine what you might do next. Where will your peacemaking journey lead you?

You may jump back and forth between planning and acting. You might even get partway through your plan and realize that you need to try something different. This peacemaking project process is not a recipe. Rather, it is a toolbox: a resource where you can pick and choose what will be most helpful. You can explore all of these tools and steps in greater depth and connect with other young peacemakers around the world at www.peacefirst.org.

After all, peacemaking is a journey and not a destination. Even though they have beginnings and ends, your peacemaking projects must be viewed the same way. All journeys start with that first step of committing to begin.

TIPS FOR GATHERING FEEDBACK

NO PLAN IS PERFECT. THIS IS ABOUT LEARNING AS YOU GO AND TAKING SMALL STEPS TOWARD YOUR GOAL. GET FEEDBACK FROM AS MANY PEOPLE AS POSSIBLE, AND ADJUST YOUR PLAN AND BUDGET AS NEEDED. HERE ARE SOME WAYS TO DO THIS:

— GATHER PEOPLE'S THOUGHTS ABOUT YOUR PROJECT BEFORE YOU START AND AGAIN AT THE END. MAKE SURE YOU USE THE SAME QUESTIONS AND ASK THE SAME PEOPLE SO YOU CAN COMPARE THEIR ANSWERS. HOW ARE THEY DIFFERENT?

— CONDUCT A SHORT SURVEY OF PEOPLE INVOLVED WITH YOUR PROJECT. IF YOU DO AN EVENT, ASK PEOPLE TO SHARE WHAT THEY LIKED BEST ABOUT IT AND WHAT THEY WOULD DO DIFFERENTLY.

— FIND OUT IF ANOTHER ORGANIZATION IS ALREADY COLLECTING USEFUL INFORMATION OR DATA (LIKE SUSPENSION OR GRADUATION RATES) THAT YOU CAN USE. LIBRARIES AND LOCAL GOVERNMENTS ARE GREAT SOURCES.

— KEEP IN MIND THAT SOMETIMES "BAD" FEEDBACK IS MORE USEFUL THAN "GOOD" FEEDBACK BECAUSE IT TELLS YOU WHAT TO DO NEXT. BE OPEN AND PATIENT. MISTAKES ARE IMPORTANT FOR SUCCESS.

PENDING DISASTERS

WHEN I WAS ten years old, I decided to bake a cake. Not just any cake. An ooey, gooey triple-layer chocolate cake whose bright, shiny picture was the highlight of the red Betty Crocker cookbook we had in our kitchen. I had done a little cooking, even making an entire dinner for my family once. But I had never baked anything before. At least not on my own. I probably should have started with something smaller, something easier. But I had my heart set on this cake. And it was important to me to do it without any adult help.

The recipe seemed simple enough, and I carefully measured out each ingredient, adding them in just the right order. I mixed the growing batter for exactly how long I was supposed to, carefully stirring until the whole mixture was the perfect consistency of chocolate goodness.

I poured the mix into three round pans, each one a bit smaller than the one before, so I could create a tiered chocolate masterpiece. I placed the pans into the oven, set the timer, and waited. And waited. And waited. It seemed to take forever.

Ding! The timer went off, I took the pans out, removed the cakes, and stacked them, neatly, one on top of the other. Then I applied heaping spoonfuls of ooey, gooey chocolate frosting to the top and sides of the cake. Then I stepped back to admire what I was sure was the most beautiful cake ever made.

I looked at my cake. Then I looked at the shiny picture in the red Betty Crocker cookbook. Then I looked back at my cake. They looked absolutely nothing alike.

You see, I had not realized that when you cook three different-size cakes you need to cook them for different amounts of time. The small top layer was a charred chocolate rock that slid to the edge of the middle layer, which had sunk into the not-fully-cooked bottom layer. And because I had been so eager to frost my cake, I hadn't realized that a hot cake needs time to cool before you put frosting on it, so all of that ooey, gooey chocolate frosting had slid into a brown puddle at the base of my cake. The cake reminded me of a chocolate *Titanic*, slowly sinking into a brown frosting ocean. It was an utter disaster.

Being a peacemaker is like this. You will do exactly as you are told, try to live every single commitment, follow each step to the detail, yet your actions will still, sometimes, end up a big mess. It will be undercooked in some places and burnt in others. It will fall apart. Sometimes it will even be a disaster. And it will look nothing like the pictures.

Throughout our lives, we are given examples of heroes who have changed the world, and we're told to be like them. But you can't be like them. You need to take your own journey. And nobody, not even the greatest, bravest, kindest peacemaker, is like that all the time. Dr. King didn't spend most of his time giving great speeches. He sat through a lot of meetings. He got grumpy and confused, and lost and lonely. Just like all of us.

All of the peacemaking stories in these chapters are told after they have happened. But they all looked very different in the moment. And your story will look nothing like the stories you've read.

The commitments in which you are engaging are not always going to be easy. The work of peacemaking is about being different in a world that is desperately trying to keep you the same. It can be hard to be different. It can feel lonely.

But a better world exists only because each of us makes it possible. It will not be easy to sustain a sense of commitment during the times of struggle that will come. When the adults in your life ignore you, or try too hard to be helpful. When you pour your heart out and someone responds with a condescending smile and "Oh, that is so cute!" When the challenge of balancing school, your project, and friendships feels like too much.

When you don't know if the peacemaking work you are doing will make any difference.

But it will.

Just like my cake, your peacemaking work may not look like a shiny picture of success. But it will have a beauty all its own. And by leaving behind a lasting piece of goodness, you will make the road a bit smoother for those who will come next. You will be a trailblazer.

And, by the way, that chocolate cake was the best I have ever eaten. Not because it was perfect. But because I made it with my own two hands.

ACKNOWLEDGMENTS

A book like this would not have been possible without countless colleagues, loved ones, and advocates. While it is impossible to name them all, there are a few I would like to thank for their advice, wisdom, support, and love.

My parents, Karen and Dick Dawson, who have reviewed just about everything I've written since I was five, provided invaluable edits and suggestions. Their commitment to social change, family, and curiosity remains my most important model. Thank you for being such powerful examples of peacemakers.

My wife, Tammy Tai, without whose generosity and encouragement this book could never have happened, provided editing support, writing time, advice, and boundless affection.

My children, Veronica, Jivan, and Xochitl, gave up countless Sundays, summer vacations, and early mornings together so that I could squeeze in writing time. I hope this book becomes something you can share with your children someday.

My talented sister, Katie Dawson, shared the pain and joy of the writing process through brainstorming, support, and the occasional glass of wine.

I am grateful for the love and support of my extended family, Jill, Drew, Joshua, and Alyssa Dawson; Bob, Lilah, and Ruby O'Dair; Maureen and John Tai; and Tawanna Fulton.

My godchildren, Curtis, Jasmine, Jalynn, Christopher, Dominique, and Donte, have been my most important teachers about how to nurture and support young people. Thank you for being my early guinea pigs.

The ideas in this book have been sanded by countless young people, educators, and colleagues who span the globe. I am grateful for your shared commitment to peacemaking.

To Anne Peretz, who plucked me off the street as a teenager, gave me a place to live, and opened up more doors than I can count.

To the memory of Dr. Francelia Butler, from whose mind and passion Peace First first sprang and who was a tireless advocate for young people's abilities to change the world.

To the memory of Dr. Steven Brion-Meisels, who, more than anyone else, shaped how I understand peacemaking, writing, and leadership.

To Lisa Graustein, who, besides being my dear friend and social justice thought partner for more than twenty years, provided critical insights into structure and exercises, and taught me how to share a keyboard.

To Dr. Jim McElligott and his wife, Ann, who were two of the first adults who took me seriously and provided a template for how to support others.

To John King, my partner in crime and best friend, who roped me into this work in the first place and taught me the importance of moral clarity and commitment, and how to best bend the long arc of history toward justice.

I am grateful to my colleagues at Peace First, past and present, who have contributed to making this book happen. I am especially grateful to Grace Bianciardi and Lauren Chamberlain, who provided early framing and feedback; Raul Caceres, Kelsey Thompson-Briggs, and Fish Stark, who shared thoughtful guidance on tools and language; Bobby Jones, Dan Cardinali, Shruti Sehra, Nancy Klavans, Jon Mandle, Karen Grant, and Jennifer Clammer for being early and vocal advocates for this project; and Renee Albanese, who provided tremendous support, organization, and good cheer.

As a first-time writer, I was unbelievably fortunate to have such a terrific team behind this project.

This book would not have happened without the gentle nudging and introductions of Dan Weiss and my agent, Amy Berkower, who made the whole process effortless.

Ken Wright at Viking believed in this book even before I did. My editor, Catherine Frank, was a true partner in crafting this project; a first-time writer could not have done better. And many thanks to John Vasile, Janet Pascal, and Kate Renner at Viking.

To my crew of young reviewers, Alyx Bernstein, Bentley Adkins, Madeline Liston, Liana Smolover, Kylee McCumber, Lilly Anne Marsh, and Andrew Shady, thank you for making sure my writing stayed true and real.

And finally, to the amazing young people who opened up their hearts and lives and shared their brave and thoughtful stories that have shaped and guided this project: Amanda Matos, Amit Dodani, Babatunde Salaam, Brennan Lewis, Danielle Liebl, Eli Erlick, Emily-Anne Rigal, Grace Callwood, Imani Henry, Isabella Griffin, Jasmine Babers, Jeremiah Anthony, Jessica Carscadden, Justin Bachman, Katebah Alolefi, Mary-Patricia Hector, Matthew Kaplan, Nicholas Lowinger, Sarah Cronk, Wei Chen, Xiutezcatl Martinez, and Yasmine Arrington. While I was unable to put each of your stories fully in the book, your wisdom forms its DNA. I am grateful for each and every one of you. You are amazing.

INDEX

Note: Page numbers in *italics* refer to illustrations.

action, taking, 9, 22–33
    adults who discourage, 23
    and deciding what *not* to do, 31
    difficulty of, 30
    and making mistakes, 28, 30
    and Matthew's bullying workshops, 25–29
    and meaningful problems, 32
    persistence in, 28
    and waiting for someone else to act, 23, 31

adults
    complicated positions of, 129–30
    discouraging peacemaking efforts, 23
    feelings of helplessness in, 30, 88
    getting support from, 27, 130
    insensitive behaviors of teachers, 35, 36, 37, 42
    lack of intervention from, 48, 49, 50, 53
    negative responses of, 17–18
    and victim blaming, 49

anger
    of author, in youth, 1
    and identifying injustices, 103
    and Mary-Pat's gun-violence campaign, 94

    and Wei's school boycotts and rallies, 50–51
    and working with one's enemies, 75, 78, 79

apologizing, 11

athletic teams, inclusive, *39*, 39–40

awareness raising, 19, 38

Baltimore Police Department, 73–79

BeOne project, *26*

billboard campaign of Mary-Pat, 88–92, 94, 95

boycotts, 47, 49–54, *52*

bullying, 24–29
    committing to intervene in, 1–2
    and creating a plan, *126*
    culture allowing, 24–25
    cyberbullying, 62–63, 107
    as injustice, 104
    and Jeremiah's positivity campaign, 61, 62–63, 65, 67
    and Matthew's workshops, 25–29

responses of adults to, 30

root causes of, *110*

solutions to, *115*, *117*

and Wei's school boycotts and rallies, 49–54

cerebral palsy, 35–36

change, slow pace of, 41

Chavez, Cesar, 15–16

Cherokee people, 2–3

choices, daily, 5, 9, 13

choosing peacemaking, 19–20

and deciding what *not* to do, 31

and Katebah's fasting relays, 15, 19

and meaningful problems, 32

persistence in, 13, 20

civil rights movement, 5

commitments to peacemaking, 8–11

audacious problem solving, 5–6

bringing others along, 10, 60–71

keep trying, 11, 84–97

opening one's heart, 9, 34–45

putting peace first, 9, 12–21

raising one's hand, 9, 22–33

small and daily, 7

taking a stand, 10, 46–59

working with one's enemies, 10, 72–83

common causes, finding, 10, 73, 81. *See also* **enemies, working with**

communication

with enemies, 76

and speaking with care, 43–44

community

building, 13, 14–18

and gun violence, 104

lack of, 15, 17, 19

working as a, 10

compassion, 35, 44, 107

connecting with others

and Danielle's programs involving people with disabilities, 40–41

and Katebah's fasting relays, 15, 16, 19, 20

and Matthew's workshops cultivating, 25–29

prioritizing, 10

courage

as many small decisions to act, 55

diverse measures of, 57

and feelings of fear, 10, 47

deciding to act for peace. *See* choosing peacemaking

dignity of other people, 9

disabilities, people with, 35–41
barriers faced by, 38, 40
and Danielle's programs, 37–41, *39, 40*
discrimination against, 107
poor treatment of, 1, 35–37
and Special Olympics, 37, 39

disasters. *See* mistakes and failures

discussions, hosting, 38

dreaming big, 32

Duncan, Arne, *90*

enemies, working with, 10, 72–83
and Babatunde's police workshops, 73–79, *77*
and safety considerations, 81
steps for, 80–81
and understanding perspectives of others, 73

events, tips for, 127

failures. *See* mistakes and failures

fasting relays, *16*, 16–19

fear and courage, 10, 47

feedback, gathering, 134

flexibility, 95

goal setting in planning projects
and creating a plan, 122–24, *125–26,* 127
and putting plans into action, 128
S.M.A.R.T. goals, 120–21

gratitude, expressing, 133

gun violence campaign of Mary-Pat, *89*
billboard campaign, 88–92, 94, 95
and injustice, 104
mistakes made in, 94
and National Rifle Association, 85, 92

heart. *See* opening one's heart

helplessness, feelings of, 30

humility, 96

immigrants, violence against, 47–54, 55

injustices
identifying, 102–5
identifying alternatives to, 113
inconveniences vs., 103–4

and opponents to peacemaking efforts, 129

and problem trees, 108–11, *109–10*, 116

refusing to accept, 11

root causes of, 106–11, *109–10*, 112

See also solutions to injustices

interviews, tips for, 111

judging others, 43

keep trying. *See* persistence

kindness, acting with, 9

King, Martin Luther, Jr., 15–16, 139

language barriers, 47, 48, 52, 54, 55

Lewis, Brennan, *27*

listening to others
and creating a plan, 124, *125–26*
in interviews, 111
opening one's heart by, 35, 43

making a difference now, 4–5

manifesto of peacemaking, 8–11
bringing others along, 10, 60–71
keep trying, 11, 84–97
opening one's heart, 9, 34–45

putting peace first, 9, 12–21

raising one's hand, 9, 22–33

taking a stand, 10, 46–59

working with one's enemies, 10, 72–83

marches, 17

media attention
and Mary-Pat's sit-in campaigns, 87–88
and Wei's school boycotts and rallies, 52

mentoring programs, 39

milestones, identifying, 123, *125–26*

mistakes and failures
and Babatunde's police workshops, 77
inevitability of, 85, 137–39
learning from, 11, 85, 94–95
and Mary-Pat's gun-violence campaign, 94
and Mary-Pat's sit-in campaign, 88
and Matthew's workshops, 28, 30
as opportunities, 95
as temporary setbacks, 96

National Rifle Association (NRA), 85, 92

opening one's heart, 9, 34–45
and caring for self, 43

and Danielle's programs involving people with disabilities, 37–41

and listening to others, 35, 43

and risk taking, 44

by speaking with care, 43–44

and taking on others' concerns, 42

opinions, sharing, 9

opposition. *See* resistance or opposition to peacemaking efforts

organizing people. *See* teams

parable of wolves fighting, 2–3

patience, 57–58, 69–70, 93, 95

peace, abstract ideal of, 6

Peace First nonprofit, 2

peacemaking projects, 99–104
  about, 99–100
  and building a team, 100
  Step 1. Choosing an Injustice, 101, 102–5
  Step 2. Understanding the Root Cause, 101, 106–11, 112
  Step 3. Imagining a Solution, 101, 112–18
  Step 4. Making a Plan, 101, 119–27, *125–26*

Step 5. Putting Plans into Action, 101, 128–31

Step 6. Reflecting on Outcomes, 101, 132–34

persistence (keep trying), 11, 84–97
  in choosing peacemaking, 13, 20
  dealing with mistakes and failures, 85, 88, 94–95
  and flexibility, 95
  keys to, 95–96
  and Mary-Pat's gun-violence campaign, 85, 88–93, *89*, 94
  and Mary-Pat's sit-in campaigns, 87–88
  in taking action, 28

perspectives of others
  changes in, 41
  trying to understand, 35, 43

planning a peacemaking project, 119–27
  checking the plan, 127
  creating a plan, 122–24, *125–26*
  putting plans into action, 128–31
  and reflecting on outcomes, 132–34
  S.M.A.R.T. goal planning, 120–21

police workshops of Babatunde, 73–79, *77*

positivity campaign of Jeremiah, 61, 63–67, *65, 66*

powerlessness, feelings of, 30, 56

problem trees, 108–11, *109–10*, 116

putting peace first, 9, 12–21
    actions to take for, 19–20
    and Katebah's fasting relays, 14–18, *16*
    persistence in, 21
    and resistance to peacemaking
      efforts, 17–18

raising one's hand. *See* action, taking

recklessness in risk taking, 130–31

reflecting on peacemaking outcomes,
    132–34

resistance or opposition to
  peacemaking efforts
    and Babatunde's police workshops, 78
    and expecting roadblocks, 129
    identifying, 116, *117*
    and Jeremiah's positivity team, 65–66
    and Katebah's fasting relays, 17–18
    and Mary-Pat's gun-violence
      campaign, 95
    and Wei's school boycotts and rallies,
      52, 55
    and working with one's enemies, 81–82

resources required for peacemaking
  plans, 123, *125–26*

risk taking
    and Babatunde's police workshops,
      76, 79
    and courage, 47
    and opening one's heart, 44
    and safety considerations, 130–31
    when taking a stand, 57
    and working with one's enemies, 79

roadblocks, 129. *See also* resistance or
  opposition to peacemaking efforts

root causes of injustice, 106–11, 112

safety considerations, 81, 130–31

setbacks. *See* mistakes and failures;
  resistance or opposition to
  peacemaking efforts

sit-in campaigns, 87

S.M.A.R.T. goal planning, 120–21

social media, 63–67, 107

solutions to injustices, 112–18
    and goal setting, 120
    helpers and opponents in, 116, *117*
    and putting plans into action, 128
    and root causes of injustice, 112
    and solution trees, 113–16, *114–15*
    tips for, 118

speakers, hosting, 38

Special Olympics, 37, 39

sports teams, inclusive, *39*, 39–40

standing up for peacemaking, 55–56.
  See also taking a stand

The Stop Bullying Club (Williams), *viii*

strategic thinking, 93

success, measures of, 124, *125–26*

taking action. *See* raising one's hand

taking a stand, 10, 46–59
  and courage, 47, 57
  helping others stand for themselves,
    56
  for ideas and beliefs, 56
  and patience with oneself, 57–58
  and risk taking, 57
  and Wei's school boycotts and rallies,
    47, 49–54, *52*
  for yourself and others, 55–56

teachers. *See* adults

teams (bringing others along), 10, 60–71
  and creating a plan, 123, *125–26*
  and expressing appreciation, 133
  guidelines for, 69–70

and Jeremiah's positivity team, 63–67,
  65, 66
and reflecting on outcomes, 133
and tips for building a team, 100
and value of teams, 61, 68

Think Twice gun violence campaign of
  Mary-Pat, 88–93, *89, 94*

Tutu, Desmond, 82

Twitter, 61, 63–67

unfairness in the world, 1, 3

Unified Sports, 39, *40*

U.S. Department of Justice, 53–54

victim blaming, 49

violence
  gun violence, 85, 88–92, 94
  against immigrants, 47–54, 55
  peacemakers' responses to, 13–18
  root causes of, 107

waiting for someone else to act, 23

Williams, Marcus, *viii*